OUR
FAVORITE
MOVIES

How Films Affect Our
Mental Health

Ann—
Thanks so much for
buying my book! I really
hope you enjoy it!
/Anne Feustel

Anne Feustel

Positively Powered

Author: Anne Feustel

Book Cover Design: Melody Christian, Finicky Designs

Editor: Amy Collette

Positively Powered Publications
Louisville, CO

PositivelyPoweredPublications.com

Ordering Information: Quantity sales. Special discounts are available on quantity purchases by corporations, associations, and others. For details, contact us at positivelypoweredauthors.com.

Photography: All photos are credited to Randy Ellis Photography unless otherwise stated.

Our Favorite Movies/Anne Feustel. — 1st ed.

ISBN 978-1-7329022-3-7

DEDICATION

For my favorite movie buddy ever, Jane
And my future movie buddy (hopefully), Hava

CONTENTS

"We all are born with a certain package. We are who we are: where we were born, who we were born as, how we were raised. We're kind of stuck inside that person, and the purpose of civilization and growth is to be able to reach out and empathize a little bit with other people. And for me, the movies are like a machine that generates empathy. It lets you understand a little bit more about different hopes, aspirations, dreams and fears. It helps us to identify with the people who are sharing this journey with us."

-Roger Ebert, Life Itself

INTRODUCTION

When it comes to the reason authors do what they do, my favorite quote is from Anaïs Nin, who said, "We write to taste life twice, in the moment and in retrospect."

This book is based on things that I love, that inform my character, that help me to heal, that teach me, and that have made me who I am. I get to experience all that over again writing this book. It isn't all fun and games, but then it would be a very boring book if it were. It's about my struggles with serious mental health issues and how I've used watching movies as a way to cope. It's about how I connect with my fellow film fans, especially my sister. It's about how researchers and mental health workers have found that watching movies can soothe people and help them learn more about themselves.

In the first section, I share my mental health journey. I talk about dealing with symptoms of depression, mania, anxiety, and psychosis. I will share with you how watching films has been a coping skill throughout my life. I'm not seeking pure escapism when I watch a movie, but something beyond that. It took rewatching *The Princess Bride* in college to have the first inkling that a movie could help me in that way. It was just a few short years ago when I came to the full realization of how positively movies have impacted my life.

The second section covers how films can heal and uplift everyone. Cinematherapy is a way to use watching movies as a way to grow, let your feelings go, and learn about yourself and others. I discuss the masterful work of cinematherapists Gary Solomon and Birgit Wolz and describe how researchers have found that cinematherapy can help both children and adults. I explore the research behind how certain movies can inspire people to be more kind, and how watching Disney movies completely changed the course of one young man's life.

The third section is all about how I picked the movies—the criteria I used and what types of reservations led me to reject some movies that might have otherwise made it into the book. I dig into those movies (and others), looking at things like fatphobia, transphobia, sexism, racism, homophobia, and violence.

In the fourth and final section I talk about 12 movies in depth: *Inside Out, Eternal Sunshine of the Spotless Mind, Fried Green Tomatoes, A League of Their Own, Defending Your Life, The Princess Bride, Big*

Business, Tommy Boy, When Harry Met Sally…, Joe Versus the Volcano, Little Women (the 1994 version), and *Contact.*

Each movie chapter includes four sections: "My Thoughts on This Movie" is my take on the movie and the characters. "How Watching This Movie Can Affect Our Mental Health" is about how the movie helped me and how it might help you. "Caveats and Triggers" are things I didn't like about the movie (if there are any) and any scenes that might trigger someone to relive a traumatic event. Think of the "Fun Facts" sections as a written form of DVD special features.

I hope that reading about my mental health journey will help you with any psychological issues you may have, even if you haven't been officially diagnosed with anything. I encourage you to choose watching movies as one of your coping skills and to think about how to choose the best movies to help you on your mental health journey. Finally, I hope that reading about the 12 movies in the book will help you in some way.

PART I

My Mental Health Journey

CHAPTER I

Half a Happy Childhood

I had half a happy childhood. There were so many good things—a stable and loving home with parents who took care of my sister and me emotionally and financially. Though we had disposable income, we were not spoiled with material things. I love the reasonably minimalistic values of my family. Experiences were more important than stuff, so we traveled a lot—including a full month on the road every other year until I was 14 when we moved from Madison, Wisconsin to Denver, Colorado. After that, we still traveled quite a bit.

We would visit various members of our extended family (who lived all over the country) fairly often over the years, and most of them would visit us as well. These were almost always lovely visits, especially with my Grandma Feustel, who we usually saw two times a year. She loved to play with me and my sister, spend time with us, and support us. Like my grandma, I have always loved to be silly and part of the fun. She taught me that it's important to revel in the joys of life whenever you can.

I have a lot of evidence of the happy times—so many photo albums full of those times that my mother put together over the years. Photos of vacation time—of goofing around with various friends and family members, and of my silly grins—all prove that there were a lot of enjoyable moments in my childhood.

The unhappy half was that I've dealt with depression, suicidal thoughts, and chronic insomnia, since I was at least 10. Ever since then, my mind sometimes will go on an endless loop of how dying by suicide would somehow fix everything. I don't remember making any concrete plans to die by suicide in childhood; that would come in my mid-teens.

I'm not sure when the anxiety started, but I think around the same time as the depression. I suffered alone for a long time. It wasn't until I was 18 that I told my parents about my mental health issues.

I have been bullied or looked down on for being overweight off and on since age 5, and just for my general weirdness since age 10. I think it was a factor in the development of my mental health issues. I didn't make friends easily, not only because of my size and eccentric nature but because I was shy and desperately afraid of kids rejecting me as a friend. I am and always have been an extremely sensitive person who is easily hurt. Don't get me wrong, I had friends most of the time, but not all the time.

There was also a genetic factor that contributed to my depression and anxiety—at least three members of my extended family were diagnosed with depression (that I know of), and at least one of them was also diagnosed with an anxiety disorder. In fact, one of those family members died by suicide long before I was born.

So, what did I do when I was feeling lonely? When I didn't have any friends or when I just felt alone in the universe? I isolated and distracted myself using two things: books and movies.

Books have been at the center of my life since I was little. I remember helping (or at least trying my best) to teach my best friend Chrissy how to read when we were in first grade. I remember reading her a book about monsters. I did a mean monster voice, all growly and scary. I would hide behind and escape through books, and still do to a certain degree. If I didn't have someone to sit with at school during lunch, I would read and ignore everyone. Over the years, reading books made me feel less alone, especially if I empathized with characters who were going through an incredibly tough time and who made me feel better about myself.

It's the same with movies. For just about anything I struggled with there was a movie that, looking back, tackled at least one of my issues. I don't remember being self-aware enough of my situation to say to myself, "You are going to feel so much better about yourself after you watch this amazing movie."

I do know for sure that movies both helped and made a distinct impression on me.

Let's start with movies about mental health. *Girl, Interrupted* and *Benny and Joon* stand out. Neither are perfect, but they feature complex characters I could relate to.

Girl, Interrupted is based on author Susanna Kaysen's memoir of her time at an inpatient psychiatric ward in the 1960s. She was admitted after she attempted suicide and was diagnosed with borderline personality disorder. She closely bonded with the other girls and women on the ward during her time there, though her friendship with Lisa Rowe, who was labeled a sociopath (now known as antisocial personality disorder), had its ups and downs. (Winona Ryder played Susanna and Angelina Jolie won an Oscar for her portrayal of Lisa.)

In *Benny and Joon*, Mary Stuart Masterson's Joon has symptoms of psychosis and anxiety and may be on the autism spectrum. Her romantic connection to the strange Johnny Depp character Sam was incredibly moving and lovely. ("Strange Johnny Depp character" describes 90% of his roles to date, but since this was arguably the second of such characters it wasn't annoyingly repetitive at that point.)

In *Tommy Boy* (see Chapter 18), I could relate to how Tommy was bullied for his weight throughout the movie. I also identify with Minnie Driver's character Benny in *Circle of Friends*. She felt unattractive and therefore completely bewildered that any boy could ever love her, especially one as handsome as the character played by Chris O'Donnell. Like myself, Benny was bullied or looked down upon for her weight her whole life.

Contact (see Chapter 22) showed me that just because I'm a nerd, it doesn't mean that I can't make friends, and that other nerds often make the best of friends.

Here's the thing about learning how you can relate to people, either real or imaginary—it can help you personally ("Gosh I feel better because someone else is like me!") and it can also make you more likely to understand another person's issues (they are being rude because they feel alone or broken in some way).

The character of Kit in *A League of Their Own* (see Chapter 14) doesn't treat her sister Dottie well because she is jealous of Dottie's looks, talent, and how she is perceived. That doesn't make Kit a terrible person; it makes her more relatable to me than Dottie because she is more flawed.

The first movie I remember watching in the theater was *An American Tail* when I was 5. I remember feeling at the time that the movie was a little bit scary. My mom had taken my friend and me to see it. My friend got so freaked out watching it she had to sit outside in the lobby and my mom had to sit with her. Mom wanted all of us to just leave, but I wasn't budging.

I remember being pissed off at my mom because I wanted to watch the movie with her. But I also had the thrill of watching it by myself and dealing with the scary stuff in a "big girl" way. I wasn't really all by myself the entire time, as my poor mom just had to go back and forth between my friend and me to make sure we were both okay. (Yes, I know, nowadays parents aren't supposed to leave their 5-year-olds alone in public for more than a minute. But this was the mid '80's in a mid-sized Midwestern city. A different era for sure, and a place where my mom knew half the city).

I find it kind of odd that I would have retained this memory for so long when there have been so many other important events that seemingly would have taken precedence. My guess as to why it is still in my noggin is that it was a formative event that shows my first glimmer of independence and my first memorable movie experience.

Since I was so shy, one of my favorite ways to "socialize" was through the communal experience of the movie theater. This may sound strange but hear me out. We are all in there together, no matter who any of us came with or if we arrived at the theater alone. Even without looking around, you can *feel* the collective laugh, the collective big intake of breath, and the matching tears.

You see, we the audience are doing this together. We are creating a shared experience.

My movie partner in crime throughout my childhood and adolescence was my younger sister Jane. Of the 12 movies I write about in Part IV, we saw at least 10 together, some of them countless times.

More than any other movie, we love to watch *When Harry Met Sally...* together (see Chapter 19), and we still quote lines to each other.

My sister and I are very different people—our personalities, people skills, and body sizes have always been opposites. In terms of our personalities, I'm introverted, dreamy, with my head in the clouds, and a terrible planner. I am all about going with the flow. My sister is extroverted, no-nonsense, detail-oriented, and likes to plan everything. As far as people skills—Jane has them in spades, and mine are limited. I've been overweight since childhood, and she has always been much thinner than me.

None of these differences mattered when we watched movies together, or at least when we were engrossed in them. We were together, in the same moment, and sharing the same experience. One of the things we do have in common is a deep sense of empathy. I think our ability to feel compassion helped us to relate to the characters more and thus be fully engaged in watching them.

Looking back, I know that even though I didn't realize at the time how much the movies were helping me, they still gave me relief from my mental health issues. I know in my heart of hearts that anything that children become overly attached to, that they go to again and again, is something that gives them solace. However, having this type of attachment can become harmful, an obsession that crowds out meaning in the rest of their lives.

I recognize that watching so many movies might have kept me from interacting more with other kids, which could have improved my people skills. However, I feel that if I had not watched movies so much, I would have found another way to isolate myself from others outside my family because of my poor social skills. (I would have likely just upped my reading time). Ultimately, I know that being a movie buff from a young age made me the person I am today, and I feel pretty good about that.

CHAPTER 2

Playing Ping-Pong on the Psychiatric Ward

Something was going on with me, but I didn't have a clue. I was a student at Cornell College (a small liberal arts college in Mount Vernon, Iowa—not Cornell University in Ithaca, New York—I may be somewhat smart, but not Ivy League smart) and it was my sophomore year.

At Cornell College, students take one course at a time for three and a half weeks. Each course is referred to as a "block." Students have four days off after every block—called a "block break"—until the next course starts.

We were on one of those breaks and I was looking for someone to hang out with, but I couldn't find anyone. I was feeling lonely and rather keyed up, so I needed some company. I left a note on a friend's whiteboard outside her dorm room to let her know that I had come by to visit. I suddenly felt the need to go to the train bridge just outside our small campus.

When I got there, I then felt that I should start climbing up the trellis on the bridge. I got about halfway up and looked down. I thought about how easy it would be just to jump. I wouldn't have to deal with the difficulties of life anymore, especially my battle with depression.

I was still looking down at the tracks and the backyards of the houses near the tracks when I heard a siren. A police car showed up, and a police officer got out of his squad car and asked me to climb down. I did so, readily.

The cop and his partner took me, sitting in the back of the police car, to a hospital. I was put in a single ER room while the nursing staff discussed me. They called me "the suicide," which felt awfully demeaning. I signed myself in voluntarily, but if I hadn't, they would have had the grounds to hold me there involuntarily.

I ended up in a mental health facility for about a week. I had what is called a "mixed episode"—when a person experiences depression and mania at the same time. When someone with bipolar disorder—which is what I have—experiences a manic episode, that person may have no impulse control, feel elated, experience insomnia but not be tired, become delusional, make unwise snap decisions, and not realize that things are going very wrong. It can be hard for another person to understand what someone going through a manic episode is saying, as the person might sound disjointed or nonsensical.

Later on, I went from mania to hypomania, another symptom of bipolar disorder that some call "mania-lite." In hypomania, unlike mania, the person experiencing the episode has a higher likelihood of being able to go about normal activities. All these symptoms might be present but in a muted quality. A person experiencing hypomania might impulsively buy something that costs $300, even if that means that they will have problems paying their bills or can't afford eating anything other than ramen for weeks or longer. A person experiencing mania might impulsively buy a $30,000 car they can't afford, which could lead to crippling debt.

Possible symptoms for clinical depression include depressed mood, loss of interest in activities, weight loss or gain, insomnia or oversleeping, fatigue, feeling worthless or guilty, problems with concentration, and suicidal thoughts, plans, and attempts.

During a severe depressive episode, people can have suicidal thoughts, but they may also feel so worn out and useless that they aren't as inclined to act on those thoughts. Most people in this state who do attempt are more likely to do so when the dark, dense cloud of depression starts to lift but is still present.

I was experiencing the following manic symptoms: I had no impulse control, was dealing with insomnia yet I had a higher than normal amount of energy, and I had no idea my mind had gone sideways. My most obvious depressive symptom was suicidal thinking. What I had gone through was labeled an attempt. I also was feeling very low, didn't really want to do anything I usually enjoyed, had trouble concentrating, and was feeling worthless.

With mania and depression clouding my mixed-up mind, I had the energy and impulse to attempt, coupled with the desire to end my life.

What was even scarier was that with the mania came psychosis. During psychosis, thoughts and perceptions are turned on their heads, and a person can have trouble understanding the difference between the real world and an imaginary one. One of the symptoms mania and psychosis have in common is delusions, but they manifest differently. With psychosis, delusions tend to be more frightening, while manic delusions tend to feel more uplifting. Hallucinations, strange speech patterns and actions, social withdrawal, and problems functioning are other possible symptoms.

I have been trying to remember if there were any symptoms of psychosis in the weeks and months before the attempt, and I'm just not sure. I think this has to do with the fact that it is easy to look back and say, "Okay, objectively this is depression, and this is mania, and this is psychosis." But I didn't even know I was going through psychosis, so it can be hard to remember if I knew what was real and what was not. I am pretty sure that my delusions scared me to death and I was having problems functioning, but I'm not sure beyond that. (Luckily, I experienced episodes of psychosis only about five times, and I haven't had any symptoms of psychosis for over 10 years now.)

I am thankful someone called the cops that night. Not only because I am alive today, but because I thoroughly enjoyed myself in the psychiatric ward. I know that sounds weird but it's true.

Most movies paint the experience of someone in an inpatient unit as the opposite of fun, to put it mildly. The most well-known (fictional) depiction of what it's like on a psychiatric unit is *One Flew Over the Cuckoo's Nest*. The head nurse (Nurse Ratched) in that movie is so vindictive that she manipulates patients and forces some to have electroconvulsive therapy (ECT), aka shock therapy, when she's angry with them. In fact, in the mid-twentieth century, some real-life mental health workers would use ECT as a punishment.

ECT is still in use, but it's much safer than it was 50 years ago. It can be very effective in treating depression, mania, catatonia, and even dementia, and is never used as a punishment anymore. Actress and writer Carrie Fisher once shared how much undergoing ECT helped her bipolar symptoms during treatment. A friend of mine told me ECT drastically changed her life for the better.

During every single visit to a psychiatric inpatient unit, my experience was more like that of the characters in the movie *Girl, Interrupted* than those in *One Flew Over the Cuckoo's Nest*. Like the main character in the first movie, I became close with the other patients in a short period of time. Also like her, I got a lot out of the therapeutic experience. I never had a Nurse Ratched-type encounter.

During the first stay and all the stays after that, I enjoyed spending time with the other patients because they seemed to understand me better than my friends and family. I loved the round-the-clock care by the staff. I relished the attention there. I adored the safety and security of the ward.

My favorite fellow patient on that first ward told me he had been a professional ping-pong player when he was younger. Whether or not this guy actually was a real-life *Forrest Gump* and had been so good he was shilling ping-pong paddles and playing in China, I still enjoyed being taught how to at least marginally increase my ping-pong skills.

The worst part of the whole thing was calling my parents and letting them know what happened. My mom wasn't the one I was really worried about—it was my dad. I was anxious for several reasons.

I've always been super close with my dad, and he really was the more nurturing of my two parents. This is not a slight against my mom. If you grow up with two parents in your life, whether they are together or apart, one of them is just going to be more maternal no matter their gender. But I digress.

The biggest reason I was nervous to tell him was because of the relative I mentioned in the last chapter who had died by suicide. That relative was his father, who died when my dad was 8. I was afraid that having another person in his life, let alone his own daughter, even attempt to die by suicide would devastate him.

I was too close to both not to let them know. I didn't even contemplate not calling them. I just didn't want to. My dad reacted the way I thought he would—he was upset and worried—enough for him to travel to Iowa right away. He took me home to Colorado after I got out of the hospital.

And he is still incredibly worried about my mental health to this day. I wish that my actions hadn't caused him pain, but there it is.

We got through it.

Oh, and if you were wondering about my mom? I don't want to say she was fine, as that sounds like she might not have cared. More like she was supportive, but not that worried. My mom is just not the type to put much energy into worrying about anything. I wish I could be that way!

When I was discharged, leaving the comfort of the ward was tough. I felt that I wasn't quite ready for the outside world. I believed that others would think I didn't belong among the general populace, even if they didn't know about my past behavior. That people could somehow tell there was something deeply wrong with me. I also felt that I wasn't ready to deal with a world that could be too harsh for me and wouldn't accept me for who I was. Being around those with negative energy was almost too much for me to bear.

Fortunately, I was able to go back to college within a month or so to start taking classes again.

The summer after my junior year in college I had another mixed episode and ended up at an inpatient unit in the Denver area. While my treatment there was helpful, I don't remember much about the experience of being in the unit. My parents encouraged me to live at home the fall semester of my senior year and attend a local university. I agreed.

In fact, even though I had to drop a course here and there, I was able to graduate from Cornell in four years and a summer. I clung on for dear life to school. Learning was literally keeping me alive and going forward.

My favorite inpatient stay was during my senior year at another inpatient unit in Iowa. That really felt like summer camp—well, it was how I wished summer camp could have been, not the actual Girl Scouts camp I went to where everyone ignored me.

Almost all the people on the unit I was in were in their late teens or early- to mid-20s. It can be common to have mostly young adults in adult inpatient units, as typically that is the time period where mental health disorders start. Since I had many contemporaries in the ward, it was easier to bond with all of them.

I wasn't having so much fun in the beginning, as I was undergoing some serious psychosis during that stay. A student nurse had been assigned to me, and her face kept morphing into different types of faces or just abstract shapes.

I had recently watched *Fight Club* and (**spoiler alert!**) I was convinced I was some kind of female Tyler Durden: that I was my bookish self by day but doing all kinds of extremely dangerous and bizarre things at night without any awareness I was doing so. This delusion spun out of a conversation with a fellow patient who thought he had seen me drinking heavily at a party I knew I hadn't gone to.

I was also afraid that someone on the unit might come into my room and hurt me, though I had no real reason to believe this.

I didn't sleep for the first four nights I was on the ward. Part of it was because I was so scared that someone would hurt me, but most of it was because of the mania and insomnia. I finally slept once the sedating drugs I was taking caught up with me.

Once my mind started clearing, I was able to better enjoy the other patients' company. I became popular on the ward. A couple of guys seemed to have crushes on me. Different people wanted to hang out with me at the same time, so I had to pick one person over the other. We watched movies, played pool and various games, and just talked with each other.

A young man who had autism and mental health issues noticed that I was freaking out over something at the beginning of my stay. He looked at me, and to distract me he started turning the lights off and on in the common room. At least I think it was to distract me. Regardless of his intention, it worked, and from time to time I think about him and how he helped me that day.

My second suicide attempt led to the fourth stay at a mental health facility. I was again in a mixed episode and decided to take around 50 ibuprofen pills late one night. Just like the train bridge episode, I had been undergoing severe depression and I had the energy to do something about it.

At that time, I was living at home, and within an hour of taking the pills I decided to tell my parents what I had done. My parents drove me to the hospital at top speed. At the ER, they didn't need to pump my stomach but instead gave me charcoal to induce vomiting. The staff monitored me, and it turned out that I didn't have any physical damage to my organs, thank goodness. That many pills probably wouldn't have killed me, but certainly could have wreaked havoc on my body.

I went back to the same Denver-area inpatient unit where I had been previously. I made friends with a middle-aged Deadhead (aka a seriously devoted Grateful Dead fan). He, along with many others, followed the band from city to city, seeing all their concerts and developed a shared community. I loved hearing his stories about the concerts and his community of lovable weirdos. (I don't use that as a derogatory term. I myself am a weirdo, and most of my favorite people on earth are also weirdos.)

What I didn't remember until nine years later when my sister reminded me, was that she was home on her spring break at the time of that attempt. How did I not remember that? Well, not only can moderate to severe mental health issues eat holes in your memories—so can the meds.

Not only had she been there, she thought that something she said had caused me to attempt. I felt so bad that she had gone through that. I told her that it wasn't her fault; that no one is ever responsible for another person's attempt. So many factors go into a person's attempt to die by suicide. The vast majority of the time the biggest factor is a diagnosed or undiagnosed mental health disorder.

Let me explain it this way. People make comments all the time that could possibly be construed as harmful. Just because someone may feel hurt by said comment, it just won't, by itself, lead to someone trying to die by suicide. But I still feel guilty that I put my sister through that pain.

If you are going through mental health issues and want to talk to someone about it, I recommend calling a crisis line. You don't need to be in desperate measures to call (or text) and it's free. The phone number is 1-800-273-8255 or you can text "talk" to 741741. You can also start an online chat with a counselor at suicidepreventionlifeline.org/chat/. If you need any resources, they can help with that too. Some states and cities have support or peer lines geared towards folks who aren't currently in crisis but still need someone to talk to. I have worked on a support line in the past, and it was one of my favorite things I have ever gotten to do.

Another option is to go to websites such as psychologytoday.com or goodtherapy.org to find a mental health professional. Through these sites you can find out which care providers in your area take your health insurance, what issues they can help people with, if they specialize in a certain age range of clients, and more.

CHAPTER 3

My Movie Epiphany

There are many definitions of "epiphany" but in this context I mean an illuminating discovery, realization, or disclosure. A "lightbulb moment" if you will. So, this chapter is about my realization that watching movies helped me more than I ever knew.

To set the scene: I was in the midst of a manic episode during my junior year of college. I couldn't sleep and wanted to fill the hours with something. I decided to watch *The Princess Bride* (see Chapter 16). It was the perfect choice—to watch *a* movie, and to watch *that* movie. It calmed me down a bit as I got lost in that movie's magical world. I had seen it countless times, so I didn't need to use much of my brain to figure out what was going on in the story. I was taken back to a world I had often visited since I was a child.

I came to this assessment from looking back on the situation, though it did stick in my head that somehow this was a good movie to watch while manic. Since then I've watched this movie many times during sleepless, manic, or hypomanic nights.

It is serendipitous that I remembered how much watching *The Princess Bride* was helpful, mental health-wise. When someone goes through a moderate to severe psychiatric episode, it can turn the brain into Swiss cheese. Cognitive thinking is so affected that it's harder to hold onto memories of things that happened during an episode. This can also be true of someone who is experiencing things like grief or intense physical pain.

During that viewing, I knew watching that particular movie at that particular time was beneficial. It was the first eureka moment I had about how a movie affected me, but it would take some time until I fully realized that watching movies had always been one of my coping skills.

What are coping skills?

They are actions you can take to deal with how you are thinking and feeling. Every person on earth uses coping skills to get through the day. Technically, just about anything that brings you pleasure, decreases physical, emotional, and spiritual pain, or helps you deal with stress can be a coping skill.

"Hmmm," you might say to yourself. "That means that some coping skills are harmful. The internet told me that coping skills are things you *should* do, like yoga and eating healthy. You mean I can do anything I want, and since it helps me feel better, then it's okay? Yahoo!"

Okay, no.

First, some coping skills are better for you than others, and all of them should be done in moderation. Second, I don't want to get sued, so double no. The only thing I would agree with in that last paragraph is that coping skills aren't about "shoulds." You are not coping with life when you are forcing yourself to do something you hate to do, or when you shame yourself for not doing something you think you "should" do. Stop shoulding all over yourself, please. (Don't get me wrong, we all must do some things we dislike. It's just that doing these kinds of things usually don't lift our spirits.)

You could theoretically use an addiction to anything as a coping skill, no matter what it is. All addictions can wreak havoc on your mind, body, and spirit, so moderation is the key. For instance, I can't watch more than about four movies a week. Otherwise, I am escaping too much from the real world while increasing my isolation time (if I'm watching the movies by myself).

I read an amazing book by one of my favorite comedians, Patton Oswalt, called *Silver Screen Fiend: Learning About Life from an Addiction to Film.* He talks about his obsession with watching movies during a four-year period of his life when he was starting to get known for his standup.

He spent nearly all his free time at movie theaters. In those four years, he went to see over 600 movies in the theaters and watched an untold number of films at home. He once saw 12 movies in two days at his favorite theater, The New Beverly. Why was he doing this?

One big reason was that he wanted to become a director and screenwriter and he believed that by watching all these movies he could attain his goals. In his book he wrote: "Look at me—aren't I a diligent soon-to-be filmmaker, doing my time in the darkness like this?"[1] Another reason? He had convinced himself that by watching all these movies, it was somehow helping him to be a better comedian (which he admits makes no sense whatsoever).

Oswalt has been dealing with severe depression since he was young, and though he doesn't directly say this, I would speculate that watching movies was one way he coped with it.

His addiction to movies negatively affected his mental state, at least one romantic relationship, his

---

[1] Oswalt 2015: 9

ability to connect with people in general, and his sleep. Luckily, he realized how his addiction to film was affecting him and has cut way down on his viewing habits, though he never went cold turkey that I'm aware of.

Interestingly, Oswalt said in his 2009 stand-up special *My Weakness is Strong* that when he's depressed one of the things he will do is "…watch *The Princess Bride* 11 times in a row." From the context and his lack of moderation, it probably wasn't helping him the way watching that movie helps me.

Strangely, watching a movie he hated was part of what turned his life around. While he was endlessly talking for days with friends about how awful he thought *Star Wars: Episode I – The Phantom Menace* was, he realized that at least the director, George Lucas, had tried to make a good movie. There were even parts that he really liked. What had he himself done other than just watch and criticize? Another realization? That he needed to find other things, like "love and food and movement, and friendships and your own work"[2] to define and motivate him. He had to stop what he was doing and find a greater purpose.

---

[2] Oswalt 2015: 161

Are you wondering if something you are doing in your life is a coping skill, or are you looking to add a new one? Google "coping skill list" and you will find 13.9 million results. I don't want to recommend just one list, as I encourage you to check out several and pick your favorites. There are also many books about coping skills if you prefer to go that route.

Did you know watching cat videos is a coping skill? Next time you go into a rabbit hole of cat videos, remember, it's good for you (in moderation)! Sometimes when I'm feeling down, I post on Facebook something like "I'm feeling depressed. Please post cat videos and pictures." I always feel better, even if people post stuff for other animals. Except pet birds, which are scary.

So why didn't I already know for sure that movie watching was one of my core coping skills? The same way that you might not realize that petting a furry friend, going for a walk, spending time with a loved one, or watching adorable kittens online can all be healthy coping skills.

It can be hard to figure out that these types of things are coping skills for two reasons: one, we might not be able to step back and observe how these things help us; and two, we might have been doing them so long, perhaps since childhood, that they have become ingrained.

It wasn't until I was 34 that I realized that not only do movies like *The Princess Bride* help me during manic episodes and sleepless nights, but that they had been helping me my entire life.

I was in training to become a peer support specialist with the Colorado Mental Wellness Network. According to their website, "Peer Support Specialists…are individuals in recovery from mental health and/or substance use disorders. They use their experience to help others seeking wellness and recovery."[3]

I had stumbled upon a section of the textbook about using humor as a coping skill when a light bulb went off in my head—*watching movies, especially comedies and comedy-dramas, were one of my main coping skills.*

It had been ingrained in my psyche that watching films could make me feel better, but I hadn't been able to fully see that. I had already been conscious that certain movies weren't good for my mental health— ones that had elements like extreme violence, and unchecked fat-shaming, racism and sexism—though I still would occasionally watch them. I sometimes

---

[3] Colorado Mental Wellness Network 2018

regret watching movies that have not only upset me or upped my anxiety in the moment, but also that take up space in my head for years (I'm talking about you, *Django Unchained*).

Once I had this awareness about the positive impact of watching movies, I put my epiphany into more purposeful action. I started being more vigilant about the movies I watched. Plus, I rewatched the ones that I remembered had brought me joy. I try to stick mostly to comedies and movies that are half comedy/half drama (aka dramedies), though there are plenty of purely dramatic films that I find especially helpful, like *Little Women* (see Chapter 21).

I also found a movie that replaced *The Princess Bride* as my go-to: *Inside Out* (see Chapter 11). This movie has been so much more beneficial to my health and well-being than any other movie I've seen.

What, exactly, do certain films do for me? Well, they uplift me. When I see a character who is dealing with the same type of issues I deal with, I feel that I'm not so alone. These characters can teach me lessons. They can show me possible paths to go down as well as why people would choose a path that I would never dream of taking. Watching an uplifting movie is so much better for me than watching one that freaks me out. It's also better than using other coping skills that aren't good for me, like comfort eating, completely isolating myself, or obsessively playing games on my Kindle.

At the beginning of this chapter, I talked about the value of getting lost in *The Princess Bride*'s created realm. I can completely immerse myself in a movie's world, which is another reason to put limits on what kind of movies I consume. I can get out of my head and into someone else's.

I not only can have the shared experience of watching a movie with someone at home or at the theater, but I also get to connect with other fans down the road. Talking it over with people is nice but quoting movie lines back and forth is where it's at.

For me, movies can feel like a warm embrace, a best friend, a way to a dream or goal, an inspiration, a parent, a teacher, a sibling, a friend, an escape, a move towards something, and an affirmation.

I hope that you, dear reader, can use movies as a coping skill as I do.

PART II

The Healing and Uplifting Power of Movies

CHAPTER 4

How Movies Can Help People

Watching films can help us be better people, improve our moods, decrease our symptoms of mental health issues, affect aggressive behavior, learn more about ourselves, and connect with others. My main focus in this section is to explore a type of mental health treatment called "cinematherapy."

What exactly is cinematherapy? It's a type of therapy where movies are used for healing and growth and can be done with a therapist, in a cinematherapy support group, or by yourself. The first person to publish on the subject was Jacob Levy Moreno in 1944. He was an incredibly influential psychiatrist and educator who felt that "therapeutic motion pictures" would help in that they were "capable of producing catharsis and helping audience members to understand themselves better."[4] He envisioned what would now be considered cinematherapy discussion groups, in which audiences would discuss how a film made them feel.

We can go even further back, to the beginning of storytelling itself, to talk about the ancient precursor of movie therapy, because that's what a movie is: a story. Stories have led to healing and growth for millennia. The ancient Greek philosopher Aristotle believed that plays could help people psychologically.[5]

In 1993 author Marsha Sinetar published *Reel Power: Spiritual Growth Through Film*. She was one of the first self-help writers to dive into the idea that movies can lead to personal and spiritual growth. According to her, "studying movies for their mystical message empowers us. We gain insight and greater self-awareness. We begin to appreciate our virtues and learn to 'see' with our heart..."[6]

While cinematherapy is the main focus of this section, I also want to talk generally about how movies can help everyone in a number of ways.

Sophie H. Janicke, an assistant professor in media psychology, writes in her article "How Positive Media

[4] Marsick, E. 2010
[5] Marsick, E. 2010
[6] Cinematherapy.com 2018

Can Make Us Better People" that she and other researchers have found that "...media with positive images and messages can make us want to become better people and help others—to become more 'prosocial.'"[7]

One study showed that meaningful films showcased "altruistic values...significantly more often than the pleasurable movies did."[8]

People felt better after they watched a movie with those types of values and even felt a pull to be kinder and more of a help to other people.

In a study Janicke co-authored, 266 students told her about films that were meaningful to them. Three of the most beloved were *Remember the Titans*, *Forrest Gump,* and *Eternal Sunshine of the Spotless Mind* (see Chapter 12).

Meaningful movies were more likely than the more trivial ones to "depict values of love, kindness, and connectedness... [and] made the participants feel more connected to dear friends and family, as well as to the transcendent spiritual aspects of life[.]"[9] Watching meaningful movies led to people being more benevolent towards others, whether they knew them or not. According to Janicke, academics have

---

[7] Janicke. 2016
[8] Janicke. 2016
[9] Janicke. 2016

found that when subjects watch meaningful movies and television programs, they think the world is a gentler and kindhearted place.

Researcher Sorina Daniela Dumtrache, in her paper "The Effects of a Cinema-Therapy Group on Diminishing Anxiety in Young People" found that engaging in the cinematherapy process can diminish anxiety. She found the lessening of anxiety significant when comparing undergraduates who were in the experimental sample (30) versus the control group (30).[10]

The young adults in the experimental sample would meet in groups of 10 and attend a cinematherapy discussion group led by a therapist. During the course of the study they watched 10 different movies together. They were encouraged to concentrate on the emotions they were feeling during the viewings and to use the experience for transformative growth. The students really loved the experience, and who could blame them?

Researchers Heewon Yang and Youngkhil Lee's "The use of single-session cinematherapy and aggressive behavioral tendencies among adopted children—A pilot study" analyzed 14 such children who had undergone severe abuse from their

---

[10] Dumtrache 2014

biological parents and were in a residential mental health program. Yang and Lee found that cinematherapy "helped the participants in the experimental group decrease their tendency to be impulsive and impatient" while "the level of the behavioral tendency toward physical aggression within the control group significantly increased after the movie night."[11]

What was going on? It seems that, like the subjects of so many other studies, the kids got a lot out of the cinematherapy group after watching *A Bug's Life*, a movie about a group of ants who are trying to deal with some aggressive bullies, a bunch of grasshoppers. When the kids were able to talk about the aggression, it seemed to help them.

When the other group didn't discuss it, Yang and Lee theorized that they "may have been reinforced by the aggressive nature of the movie and may have learned to be more aggressive, especially in [a] physical way." It seems that some modeling was going on here.

The first time I heard of the documentary *Life, Animated*, I knew I had to see it. It would be two years before I got the chance, but it totally lived up to the hype. Directed by Roger Ross Williams, it is about a

---

[11] Lee & Yang 2005: 1

young man, Owen Suskind, who is autistic and working towards independence from his parents. While we watch him prepare to move into his own apartment in an independent living facility, we hear and see the story of how Owen came to be so well adjusted.

The movie was inspired by the book *Life, Animated* by Owen's dad, Ron Suskind, about how the whole family was affected by Owen's life experience. Some of the things I refer to come from the movie and some from the book.

When he was a young child, Owen seemed locked inside his head, hardly ever saying anything coherent. A huge fan of Disney movies, he would quote a few words occasionally, and could string a few words together sometimes (like the phrase "hold you." [12])

That all changed when he was 6. After seeing his brother looking sad on his birthday, he told his parents that he thought that his brother didn't want to grow up, just like how Mowgli from *The Jungle Book* and Peter Pan felt.

His parents became very excited as not only was this his first complex sentence, but it also showed that Owen could be more empathetic than your average 6-year-old.

---

[12] Suskind 2014: 36

Later that night, his dad, came up with an idea. He saw Owen sitting on his bed and decided to see what would happen if he used a puppet of Iago, a Disney character from *Aladdin*, to talk to Owen in Iago's voice. For those who haven't seen the movie or don't remember it well, Iago, an evil parrot voiced by Gilbert Gottfried, is the sidekick to the villain Jafar. Owen and "Iago" had an interesting conversation, and Ron learned more about how his son was doing emotionally—not well—than he ever knew before.

When he was 10, Owen's parents were told by a school administrator that since he wasn't progressing enough socially at his elementary school for kids with special needs he could no longer attend the school. He was happy there, especially because he had made some good friends. When he was told about the situation, he turned to something to cope with his sadness at leaving behind his friends: drawing Disney sidekicks. He drew 100 of them, from Iago to Mrs. Potts (the teapot in Beauty and the Beast) to Rafiki (the wise monkey in The Lion King). He wrote in one of the sketchbooks: "I Am The Protekter [sic] Of Sidekicks" and "No Sidekick Gets Left Behind."[13]

He felt like a sidekick—a supporting player, but never the main hero. He thought and talked a lot

---

[13] Suskind 2014: 101

about a story about protecting sidekicks over the years, and in his early 20s he was able to write the final draft of the story. In the documentary, we, the audience, get to see an animated version of his story, which is so deep and emotionally complex that I would be proud to have written it myself.

Fast-forward to the present, and in my favorite scene, we see Owen leading a Disney club that he started in his school for young people with autism. Owen's friend, actor Jonathan Freeman, who voices Jafar in *Aladdin*, is there and reading a scene from the movie, with Owen playing Iago. Suddenly Gilbert Gottfried crashes the party, and everyone loses their minds. The joy and excitement on Owen's face are priceless when he sees Gottfried for the first time. Throughout the movie, you will often see Owen muttering to himself, not using his normal voice, but that of various Disney characters. The voice he seems to use most often sounds like Iago's.

Owen's story is about the power of movies—they can help us feel better and less alone and help us connect with other people. They can bring joy and understanding to every single viewer. I know they have done that for me.

CHAPTER 5

Gary Solomon: "The Movie Doctor^{TM}"

Psychologist and social worker Gary Solomon has written three books on cinematherapy: *The Motion Picture Prescription: Watch This Movie and Call Me in the Morning*, *Reel Therapy: How Movies Inspire You to Overcome Life's Problems*, and *Cinemaparenting: Using Movies to Teach Life's Most Important Lessons*.

Like many, Solomon has used movies as a coping skill throughout much of his life. He grew up with an abusive father and started watching movies at around 5 years old to emotionally flee the toxic reality of his home. Films would keep dread at bay, if only for a brief period. Movies taught him how to believe in others, understand them, and even love them—something his parents never taught him. From what I understand, he is not alone in having been basically raised by films.

In his mid-30s Solomon was making oodles of money and he didn't care about anything but making more. When he lost most of his money at 37, things went downhill emotionally. He wasn't using his beloved movie-watching coping skill anymore. Instead, he had turned to an array of addictions, including to various substances, food, and toxic relationships.

He realized that he needed to get back on a better path and decided to set himself a course of cinematherapy. Watching movies comforted him and helped him understand how he had fallen into his addictions. Several of the movies that featured characters whose addictions had destroyed them showed him that he needed to go into recovery. It was at that point he realized that he might be able to help others heal through cinematherapy, too.

I can relate to Solomon. As I write this book, I am the same age—37—as he was when he had his movie epiphany moment. It was only a few years ago when it dawned on me how dear and helpful movies are to me. (However, I've never made oodles of money and I doubt I ever will. I can only imagine what being wealthy would be like. I'm thinking rich enough to swim in a giant room of gold coins, a la Scrooge McDuck in the TV show *Duck Tales*.)

During his internship while attending a Master of Social Work program, Solomon found that his clients really resonated with this type of therapy. Whether they were struggling with things like grief, their own addictions, or painful memories of past romantic relationships, Solomon could find a movie that would help them. Watching the movies would facilitate certain emotions to come to the surface. The experience would also shine a light on the destructive thinking that was holding them back or show them how some characters were able to triumph against all odds.

"My clients reported seeing themselves in the movies. The more I prescribed, the better they became, and the more quickly they healed. They came out of denial and the recovery process moved much more quickly than I had anticipated, certainly faster than my peers reported they were experiencing with their clients." [14]

Solomon urges his readers to allow themselves to become fully immersed in any film so that they can get the most out of it, and I agree with him. Through this immersion, you may start to see reality, accept it, and let go of any misconceptions you have about yourself or others. He also stresses that a big part of this type of therapy is journaling about your feelings and thoughts around each movie.

<hr>

[14] Solomon 1995: 4

He urges mental health workers and those who work in the addiction, correctional services, and education fields to adopt cinematherapy practices with those they serve. Solomon regularly speaks with people serving time, teaching them how to use cinematherapy.[15] The use of this powerful tool can help them come to terms with what happened in the past that led to their incarceration and know what to avoid when they are released from prison.

In all three of his books he talks about how cinematherapy can be great for people of all ages, and in *Reel Therapy* he discusses how watching *E. T.* with your kids can be beneficial for the entire family. If you've seen the movie, you know it's a pretty darn emotional one. For parents who have a tough time expressing their feelings, Solomon recommends that they allow themselves to let the tears run or otherwise visually show how they are reacting to the movie. This way they can let their children know that there's nothing wrong with crying or becoming emotional, at least during a movie.

In his three books, he describes a total of 510 movies that he feels would be especially helpful to his readers. He includes three of the movies that are covered in this book: *Fried Green Tomatoes*, *When Harry Met Sally...*, and *Defending Your Life*.

---

[15] Mann 2007

My favorite part of each movie selection is the "Healing Themes."[16] Some of the healing themes in *Defending Your Life* are: "Taking a look at the past... If someone passes judgment on you... [and] Having to explain your actions." I am in complete agreement with Solomon that focusing on these themes can be therapeutic.

Solomon suggests that since men with mental health issues may decide that, even though they need it, they won't attend talk therapy because of the stigma attached to it, cinematherapy could feel like a safer alternative. I love this idea!

I've done research about men and depression for other projects I've worked on. Did you know that men die by suicide three and a half times more often than women do? That one in eight men will battle clinical depression sometime in their lives? Mainstream society doesn't often "allow" men to express emotions like sadness as supposedly it's a sign of weakness, though anger and apathy are more accepted.

Solomon didn't really talk about it, but I will bet dollars to donuts that he struggled with talking about his mental health issues and used cinematherapy before talk therapy. He never mentions in his books whether he saw a therapist at any point in his life. This

_____

[16] Solomon 1995: 62

is just conjecture, but it is certainly plausible that he was afraid of the stigma himself.

In a nutshell, Solomon took his own personal healing cinematherapy experience and was able to parlay that into helping his clients, readers, and others he has worked with to heal as well. He shows that through immersion in the movie experience, allowing emotions to come to the surface during the process, shining a light on detrimental thought patterns, and modeling triumphant character arcs, people can benefit greatly from following his Motion Picture Prescription.

CHAPTER 6

Birgit Wolz: "The Shadow Master"

(Since Solomon has branded himself as "The Movie Doctor™", I thought I would give Wolz a fun name as well, and since so much of her work is about embracing the shadow self, I thought "The Shadow Master" was appropriate.)

Author of the book *E-Motion Picture Magic: A Movie Lover's Guide to Healing and Transformation* and creator of what is considered the best and most comprehensive website on movie therapy, *cinematherapy.com*, Wolz has built on Solomon's (and others') work, but in my opinion took it to a whole new, exciting level.

Cinematherapy, in general, is categorized under the umbrella of cognitive behavioral therapy (CBT). One of the two most popular types of therapy in the U.S., it focuses on changing negative thoughts patterns and behaviors, which in turn positively affect emotions and create a road to recovery from mental health issues.

(In case you were wondering, the other type of popular treatment is psychodynamic therapy, which focuses more on insights and the unconscious mind and is Sigmund Freud-ish).

In my opinion, Wolz's work is more aligned with dialectical behavior therapy (DBT), which "emphasizes individual psychotherapy and group skills training classes to help people learn and use new skills and strategies to develop a life that they experience as worth living. DBT skills include skills for mindfulness, emotion regulation, distress tolerance, and interpersonal effectiveness."[17]

I've gone through both CBT and DBT, and I've found the latter to be infinitely more helpful to me. CBT is about changing your "negative" thoughts and actions. To me, this approach implies that there is something *really* wrong with me. I believe that CBT tells me that I'm broken and I must fix myself. However, I will say that undergoing that type of therapy in the past was beneficial at the time because it helped me to be more introspective. Plus, it opened my eyes to some of my distorted thinking. It just isn't useful for me anymore. To be clear, I am not saying that CBT is bad or that you shouldn't engage in it, just that it doesn't work for me now.

---

[17] Behavioral Tech 2018

DBT focuses on improving skills that can help life be more bearable and enjoyable. Also, similar to Wolz's focus on cinematherapy discussion groups, the group work is very important. My favorite part of the therapy is the emphasis on mindfulness. I've been practicing it in one form or another since I was a child, and it helps me more than anything else. Mindfulness is also a focus of Wolz's work.

Wolz, like Solomon and me, has used movies as a coping skill since she was young. She saw her first movie in a theater, *The Last Days of Pompeii*, with her grandfather when she was 7. She felt completely caught up and exhilarated by the experience, and she and her grandfather "became movie buddies".[18] A shy girl, she suddenly felt emotionally strong enough to try and make friends after being encouraged by the heroes' bravery in the movie.

In her 30s, after earning a Ph.D. in Economics, Wolz suffered a stroke, which she thought would wipe out any chance of achieving her life goals. It also severely affected the relationships in her life. She fell into a deep depression, but she couldn't cry even though she thought doing so would help her feel better. Like Solomon, she set herself a course of cinematherapy.

---

[18] Wolz 2004: 8

Watching heart-wrenching films helped her to cry, feel less alone in her struggles, and remind her that many had it worse than she did. She was inspired by the bravery of people in these movies, just as she had been inspired by the characters in *The Last Days of Pompeii*.

Wolz describes her practice as using films in "three different ways: *Prescriptively* (using films to model or illustrate specific desired qualities or behaviors), *Evocatively* (using films for self-discovery), [and] *Cathartically* (using films to find emotional release)."[19]

Remember when I said that Wolz was building on Solomon's work? It seems rather obvious that since his book is titled *The Motion Picture Prescription,* his focus is on using movies *prescriptively*. Both authors talk about immersing yourself in the movie, using movies to help change negative ideas about yourself or others, as well as showing how to overcome obstacles gracefully. Wolz also goes into detail about how cinematherapy can lead to higher self-esteem.

Using films *evocatively* is a little more interesting and is the most helpful to me of the three. If I could somehow observe my mind from a distance for, say, a week, it would be so wonderfully amazing. I would love to get into all the nooks and crannies, and even take a Dustbuster to certain old false beliefs about

---

[19] Wolz 2004: 15

myself that still kick in sometimes. It would also be scary-interesting to dig into the dark ideas and emotions that I try to hide in my head. I would like to learn more about all the things that have made me *me*.

Back to DBT: one of the skills is called "observing," which is what self-discovery is—observing what is going on inside your head. Wolz talks about how understanding "the negative traits we see in the characters or their behavior could be part of our own repressed 'shadow' self."[20] In *E-Motion Picture Magic*, she talks about how important it is to understand one's shadow self and fully integrate it into one's personality. That way, a person doesn't feel they have a good self or a bad self, but just a self. On the flip side, she discusses how helpful it is for people to determine which characters they admire. Through this process, they can learn and own the best parts of themselves.

Remember how Wolz talked about how she couldn't cry on her own at a certain point in her life, but could through watching movies? That's using films *cathartically*. What does cathartic mean? According to the Oxford English Dictionary, it means "providing psychological relief through the open expression of strong emotions; causing catharsis."

---

[20] Wolz 2004: 128

Do you need to laugh or cry because of something stuck inside? Perhaps you are worried that you're not "allowed" to express joy or sadness around other people, so letting yourself feel them while watching a movie at home is an easier or safer place to do that.

The biggest difference between Solomon's books and *E-Motion Picture Magic* is that his books are more like movie guides, and Wolz's book is more of a workbook. She has created over 60 exercises for the reader, some linked to specific movies. The exercises are based on topics such as: "Acknowledging Positive Qualities"[21] and "Acknowledging Perceived and Real Shortcomings"[22]. She focuses on 46 films in the book, though she has a long list of recommended movies in the back.

Like Solomon and me, Wolz is a fan of *Defending Your Life*, which is about the afterlife and living out of fear. She created this exercise based on the film's themes: "Remember a situation in your life when you faced a fear and pursued something of which you were afraid. You might want to try it again, starting with something small and manageable."[23]

Both Wolz and Solomon make it very clear that those who really need to work with a therapist should

---

[21] Wolz 2004: 137-138
[22] Wolz 2004: 140-141
[23] Wolz 2004: 87

do so. They acknowledge that it isn't always possible for people to get such therapy, but both authors make it clear that cinematherapy is not the same as talk therapy. Wolz points out that when certain movies intensely trigger a person to relive a traumatic event, it is essential for that person to see a therapist.

Her warning/admonition is one of the reasons why I write about possible triggers—if there are any—in the movie-specific chapters. I would also point out that in general, if you are worried about certain movies triggering you, it is of the utmost importance to do some research *before* you watch them. (I know there is a lot of controversy around whether trigger warnings "should" be pointed out at all. I thought they might be helpful for some people, so that's why I included them).

If you don't have any experience with triggers, these are things that can cause a person to relive a past traumatic event. For instance, in *Fried Green Tomatoes* there are scenes that depict domestic abuse. Someone who has gone through that type of situation might see the scenes and feel like all of a sudden they are back in the pain of the abuse.

While I watched a lot of movies with others during my psychiatric inpatient stays, I don't recall participating in any kind of organized cinematherapy. Looking back, I think watching the movies calmed me.

I remember specifically being upset in my most recent stay that there wasn't an available television we could use to watch movies. I wish that during my years in mental health treatment that I could have worked with someone in the field who knew about cinematherapy and shared that knowledge with me.

I think Wolz's biggest contribution to the field of cinematherapy is the idea that there are three ways to use the practice to help yourself: prescriptively, evocatively, and cathartically. You can pick which method is right for you, at least on that particular day; let yourself feel what you need to feel; understand all parts of you, even it freaks you out; or allow movies to wash over you.

PART III

How I Picked the Movies

Spoiler Alert! In the rest of this section I'm going to talk about something I call the "ick factor" in the following movies: *Tommy Boy, Shallow Hal, Mrs. Doubtfire, Tootsie, Sixteen Candles, Pulp Fiction, Django Unchained, Crocodile Dundee, Rocky II, The Hunger Games* series, and *Transformers*. I wanted to warn you since reading this section might spoil your enjoyment during future viewings of these movies. To be clear, some of them have more glaring issues than others. If you don't want to read about my qualms surrounding these movies, you may want to skip ahead.

CHAPTER 7

The Ick Factor Equation

The most simplistic answer to how I picked the 12 movies in this book is they were the ones that 1) I felt the best watching, and that 2) I felt had little to none of what I call the "ick factor." As for the first part, these are movies that affect at least one of the three broad types of mental health symptoms I deal with: depression, anxiety, and mania. As for the second part, when I say "ick factor" I mean movies that fit the saying "I love this movie, but I hate _____ about it."

Obviously, I needed to rewatch all the movies I was considering for this book. I thought to myself during each viewing: is this a movie I would recommend wholeheartedly, or do I have some reservations about it?

If I felt even a tad uneasy, I dug in, did some research on the movie, and decided whether I should include it. I did this intuitively, not using a spreadsheet or mathematical equation. It's kind of hard to quantify the ick factor.

One of the things I wanted to do in my preliminary research was to determine what puts me off some movies. I decided that the main things would be unchecked fat-shaming, racism, sexism, ableism (discrimination against those with disabilities and/or mental health issues), homophobia, transphobia, and xenophobia (fear or dislike of people from other countries). I also took extreme violence in movies and either depicted or implied sexual assault and abuse into account.

There were other things that kept certain movies out of the running. Maybe they were not as good as I remembered or they just didn't grab me enough to justify adding them.

Dear reader, I have a warning for you. Unless you want to discover the ick factor in as many movies as possible, don't do the research I did for this section. For example, don't Google "the most racist movies of all time" unless you are completely sure you want to know which movies are likely to show up. And don't do this type of research for any of the other ick factor qualifiers I mentioned if you aren't positive you really want to know. I found it depressing to find out this information. It was like looking at the sun for too long: too much knowledge can be painful. I lost some of my innocence in this process.

That said, what I gained through doing the research was empathy for people who have much different experiences than my own. While I have experienced things like fat-shaming and ableism, I have never experienced things like racism or transphobia. As I read through the many online pieces on the most racist movies of all time, I would be in disbelief sometimes. "I love that movie! It can't be racist! I don't remember any racism! This writer doesn't know what they're talking about!"

Then I went back and rewatched two of them and thought, "Oh—would I like to be treated like that character was? No."

Before I write about movies that didn't make the cut due to things like perceived "isms" and phobias, I want to make something clear. I am not telling anyone else that enjoying the movies I'm going to discuss makes them a bad person. I still watch movies with some ick factor involved. I might not enjoy them as much as I used to, but I in no way shape or form think anyone is a racist, sexist, ableist, homophobe, transphobe, or fatphobe for watching these movies. The same goes for the people involved in making the movies I talk about in this section (well maybe one director). An aim of mine, however, is through rewatching, researching, and writing about certain movies, to point out how the ick factor can sometimes be hiding in plain sight.

Am I a delicate flower who is too P.C. to just let this stuff go? Don't most movies have some element to them that could be questionable? To be honest, I'm very sensitive. I also believe that I know for myself which movies I want to put in my brain and to recommend to others. I included a section titled "Caveats and Triggers" in each movie entry to point out parts that I think have a slight ick factor to them (caveats) and parts that could potentially negatively affect those with trauma in their past (triggers).

The Perfect Movie: *Inside Out*

If there ever was a no-brainer movie to include, it would be *Inside Out* (see Chapter 11). It is my favorite movie of all time, and I try to encourage everyone I know to see it. There is no part of that movie that made me question its utter perfection. It's a deep and satisfying movie about how important it is to feel a full range of emotions. It's a movie for all ages, which means that both kids and adults can reap the mental health benefits of watching this movie.

I watch it when I'm depressed, anxious, hypomanic, or manic. I feel better and at least a bit more at peace with myself when watching this movie. I always cry at least once and laugh countless times, so it's good for emotional release. I feel less alone after watching this movie. It reminds me that everyone has emotions like joy, sadness, and fear. If I experience these emotions to diagnosable extremes, that's okay. It just means two things: I need to take care of myself, and, like a certain character, I have more empathy because of my experience with intense highs and lows.

Unlike some animated films, in this movie females and males are on equal footing. No female character is aiming to marry a prince—or anybody really. There are no isms or phobias—no racism, sexism, ableism, homophobia, transphobia, xenophobia or fatphobia. There is no violence either, depicted or implied.

I'm not the only one who feels this movie is perfect for improving mental health symptoms. I've seen pieces all over the internet that suggest it could improve things like depression and anxiety. MIT scientist Rana el Kaliouby who has "been studying, simulating, implementing, measuring and analyzing emotions for the past 15 years" believes that "the greatest value this movie brings is that it makes it 'cool' to talk about emotions and feelings." [24]

El Kaliouby is amazed at how the movie has inspired so many, even children, to really speak from their hearts about how they are feeling. It also gives

---

[24] el Kaliouby 2015

kids a framework for how to talk about things like anger that they might not fully understand.

CHAPTER 8

Fatphobia, Sexism, and Transphobia

Tommy Boy: Not Perfect, But Worthy

I have adored Chris Farley since I first saw him on *Saturday Night Live* in 1990. He has always been able to make me laugh uncontrollably. I loved almost every character he did, but my favorite characters were Matt Foley, a motivational speaker; a dancing lunch lady who was in love with Sloppy Joe; and a wannabe Chippendale's dancer. Chris Farley's comedic talent was unbelievable. I'm not alone in my admiration for Farley. He had, and still has, many ardent fans, both regular folk and some of the most famous comedians from the '90s to today.

Farley's skits and movies often included fat jokes, which mostly involved physical humor. In the Chippendale's sketch, he and Patrick Swayze play two men who are trying out to be male exotic dancers. The joke is that it would be ridiculous for a large man, like Farley was, to be hired as a dancer. The thing with Farley, however, was that he and the writers of his skits and movies were so talented that he could make you root for him even in these kinds of "ridiculous" situations. Those who made fun of his characters were sometimes seen as real jerks, and just because he was chubby didn't mean that making fun of him was okay.

Am I making these observations because I have always identified with him? Do I view his comedy through my own unique perception and therefore feel that there is some nuance to those skits and movies? There's no way for me to know this for sure, as I can't exactly step outside myself enough to see this completely objectively.

So, we come to *Tommy Boy* (see Chapter 18), my favorite of Farley's starring vehicles. He plays a sweet but clueless guy who needs to sell hundreds of thousands of car parts to keep his family's plant from closing. There are a lot of fat jokes in that movie and most of them are made by David Spade's character, Richard, who acts like a real douchenozzle in the movie. Some mean kids also berate Tommy during one scene. We are made to feel bad for Tommy here, as he is obviously embarrassed. Luckily for him, his friend Michelle threatens the kids with bodily harm and they run away.

Tommy makes jokes about his own weight, and there is some physical humor around his size. To me, those jokes are used as self-deprecating humor, and the people involved in the making of the movie are not trying to cast him in a negative light because of his weight.

Why am I recommending this movie to you? Well, as I said, I think it is incredibly amusing. Another reason is that, if you are overweight, you might be able to relate to Tommy and realize how those people who have been and may still be making fun of you or others are being jerks. They may have their own discernable reasons for being jerks like Richard does, but for goodness' sake, know that you are as worthy of love and appreciation as anyone else.

Finally, if you aren't and haven't ever been overweight, I invite you to watch this movie while putting yourself completely in Tommy's shoes. You might gain some perspective on what it's like to be overweight in the world today.

Almost all movies and plays have tropes, which are common or overused themes or devices. The trope of the funny heavyset (and usually dim-witted) man has been around since at least Shakespeare's time, so Farley's ongoing roles are part of a centuries-old trope. Comedians—from silent-era film star Roscoe "Fatty" Arbuckle to modern-day actor Kevin James— have been in countless movies where they played this type of character. These actors may play characters with names like Chubby, Chunk, or House. They are there for humor, and almost always are the butt of verbal and physical jokes.

Farley died alone, at 33, in a hotel room, after an overdose of heroin and cocaine. Reportedly, his physical health problems likely played a role in his death as well. His self-esteem was cripplingly low, mostly because of his weight, but also because he thought he was stupid (I've seen multiple interviews of Farley where he called himself dim-witted). Since he was a kid he visited "fat farms" to lose weight, sometimes with his father who also struggled with his weight for much of his life. In addition, he went to rehab 17 times in the last two years of his life but was never able to kick his drug habit for very long. Would we still have him if he didn't see the need to self-medicate because of how he felt about himself? I don't know for sure, but I think we would. He had such an impact in the short seven years he was on TV and in movies.

Though some people think fat-shaming is a motivator to shed pounds, it does not lead to people losing weight. In fact, according to numerous studies, it tends to lead to kids and adults gaining weight. I know during the times I felt the stigma most acutely I tended to eat more to comfort myself.

I tend to gravitate more towards overweight people as we share a similar experience of being shamed. There is more societal pressure on women to be thin or "healthy," but men feel it as well. All of us who are overweight have a fraction of the clothing options that "healthy" people have. I would wager that unless they are living under a rock, overweight people have been fat-shamed at least once, but more likely multiple times in their lives. This can come from family members, friends, peers, strangers, societal expectations, and the media.

Shallow Hal: A Double Dose of Fat-Shaming and Sexism

I've watched *Shallow Hal* many times and loved what I thought of as the message of the movie: that it doesn't matter if you are chubby, what matters is what's in your heart. Jack Black (a heavyset actor) plays Shallow Hal, who only wants to date women who are conventionally beautiful and thin. Tony Robbins (playing himself) performs some magic on Hal so that he will only see the inner beauty of all the women he meets, regardless of their actual physical appearance. Enter Gwyneth Paltrow's character Rosemary, who looks to Hal like a thin, beautiful woman, but she is really a plus-size, beautiful woman. (Paltrow dons a fat suit for the times when we see Rosemary's real self. Don't even get me into the subject of how demeaning fat suits are. Yuck.)

Doing research for this book, I Googled "fatphobia in movies" and found that Lauren Gordon of *Revelist*, Ashley Reese of *Gurl*, Jenni Maier of *Alloy*, and a number of other writers thought that *Shallow Hal* was incredibly fatphobic.

After reading these articles, I was chagrinned. The authors state that the underlying message is that a chubby woman would look like Gwyneth Paltrow if she was beautiful inside—but would not look like herself. This message tells those of us who are plus-size that we can't physically be beautiful.

What I had overlooked before, because I enjoyed the movie, were the ridiculous and offensive sight gags that supposedly "show" that Rosemary is plus-size. She does a cannonball into a pool and so much water splashes up that a boy who is swimming is launched into a tree. She breaks a solid steel chair and a very sturdy booth by sitting on them. There's more, but I am getting depressed and angry just writing this.

If you have seen both *Shallow Hal* and *Tommy Boy*, you might call me hypocritical. Didn't Tommy break a bench in the movie? Aren't there plenty of sight gags based on Tommy's weight? Yes, but I would say Farley's gags are more believable, and that was already part of his comedy since he started out in the business.

Hal is always given weird looks or laughed at when he talks about how beautiful Rosemary is. His best friend, Mauricio, goes out of his way to break them up because he hates Rosemary because of the way she looks and thinks there's something deeply wrong with Hal for wanting to date her.

What it comes down to is a math problem. You can't have the message of the movie both ways. You don't get to keep talking throughout the movie about how beauty comes from within while also including the sight gags I talked about. Don't imply that women can't be beautiful unless they look like Gwyneth Paltrow—who weighs less than half of what Rosemary does.

This is not only a dangerous notion for the world at large, but for film actresses in particular. This has been true for around a 100 years. Actresses who want to work in movies have had to deal with resorting to extreme measures such as starvation diets and life-threatening surgeries so they can be as thin as possible. The intense body shaming can lead to all kinds of mental health issues, especially eating disorders. When Jennifer Lawrence gets fat-shamed, things are looking very bleak indeed for those of us who are overweight.

Mrs. Doubtfire and the Disturbing Transphobia in Films

One movie that I thought about including but decided not to is *Mrs. Doubtfire*. In this movie Robin Williams is man-child Daniel, an out-of-work actor who is incredibly irresponsible. His wife starts divorce proceedings against him and he is given partial custody of their three kids. Heartbroken that he could only rarely see them anymore, as he had been their primary caregiver, he hatches a plan to become their new Scottish nanny. He enlists the help of his gifted makeup artist brother to design a mask so he will appear as an older woman. Donning the mask, a wig, a body suit, a dress, and sporting a Scottish accent, he meets with his ex-wife, presenting himself as a superb nanny named Mrs. Doubtfire. She hires him for the job.

I know that there are many movies out there where men dress in drag for a practical reason, not because they fall under the transgender umbrella. These movies are overwhelmingly comedies where the message is: it's hilarious when a man dresses as a woman! It's so funny when straight men fall in love with them! If those straight men find out that the cross-dressing man is not a woman, they tend to freak out and in some movies like *Tootsie*, they make threatening comments.

Spoiler alert! There are some exceptions where the straight men seem okay with the situation, like in *Some Like It Hot*, where the two main characters, Joe and Jerry, dress in drag to hide from the mob who are trying to kill them. One character, Osgood, asks Jerry to marry him when Jerry is in drag, and when he finds out Jerry is not a woman, he doesn't seem to care.

In *Mrs. Doubtfire*, when the son, Chris, sees "Mrs. Doubtfire" pee standing up, he freaks the heck out. Before finding out that his dad is the person behind the mask, the boy wants to call the police, beat up whoever this stranger is who he thinks is pretending to be a woman, and uses transphobic language.

Anne, you might say, wouldn't some kids, or at least '90s kids, be freaked out if they found out their seemingly female nanny peed standing up? Isn't this scene more realistic the way it is? I understand the point, but that doesn't mean that what happens in the movie isn't hurtful to transgender people and that I wish it had been written differently. I've seen several articles and threads online by people who are transgender who felt upset after watching the movie. There are also other scenes that reinforce the transphobia in the film.

I really did love this movie in the past with all my heart, and there are still things I enjoy about it. Ever since I was small, I have been a huge Robin Williams fan. From his roles in movies like *Aladdin* and *Good Morning Vietnam* to his televised standup specials, to raising funds for the homeless through the Comic Relief Campaign (and more) there is so much I loved about the man. I was torn as to whether I was going to write about this movie here. However, if I'm going to be my authentic self, I must be able to call out any film that has a significant ick factor, no matter who stars in it.

CHAPTER 9

The Worst Offenders

Sixteen Candles: Racism, Gay Slurs, Ableism, Xenophobia, and Probable Sexual Assault (Trigger Warning)

Birth of a Nation (1915), a pro-slavery, pro- "racial purity" film, is widely thought of as the most racist movie of all time. However, what I thought of as some of my favorite movies also contain an extreme amount of unchecked racism and racist stereotypes.

Sixteen Candles, about Sam, a teenage girl whose family completely forgets her birthday because of her sister's wedding, is one of my former favorite films. Sam is in love with a popular and good-looking classmate who seems unattainable.

Long Duk Dong, an exchange student who lives with Sam's grandparents, is a disturbingly racist and xenophobic stereotype. When he enters a scene, there is always a gong noise. He's called an Asian slur several times. Everything he says or does is played for laughs, and almost all the jokes have to do with his race.

Pieces from *NPR*, *The New York Post*, *The Guardian*, *Business Insider*, *The Washington Post*, *The Huffington Post*, and from at least 20 bloggers have covered the racism in this movie. Many of these pieces also cover the probable sexual assault in the movie.

Jake Ryan, Sam's love interest, is tired of his current girlfriend. He "gives" her when she is drunk and unconscious to the socially awkward Ted (also known as The Geek) and tells him to have fun. The Geek drives her around in a car, tries to take a photo with her as proof he went out with her, and then we see both of them wake up in the car in a parking lot the next morning. She doesn't know who he is and neither of them remembers for sure if they had sex (presumably because both of them were blackout drunk), but she thinks he had sex with her while she was passed out. She doesn't seem to mind it, and she actually wants to date him.

Just in case this wasn't enough, gay slurs are used, and a girl in a scoliosis brace is constantly the butt of sight gags that involve her wearing said brace.

Pulp Fiction and *Django Unchained*: Extreme Violence and Racism

As anyone who has watched *Pulp Fiction* and *Django Unchained* knows, these movies are as violent as they come, and the n-word is used frequently. The director of both films, Quentin Tarantino, is well-known for the extreme violence in his movies, and for his liberal use of that word. In *Pulp Fiction* it is used 21 times, and in *Django Unchained* it was used 110 times. I used to love *Pulp Fiction* and still like parts of it, but I quit watching it once I became more and more uncomfortable with the racial slurs.

Since I am not black, I don't know what it's like to have that word thrown at me or how much that might hurt. I wonder if it's even my place to be so bothered by the word. Ultimately, it's a word I don't like hearing, like the other slurs in the movies in this chapter.

I know that if I cut out all media with racial slurs I would be missing out on some of my favorite stand-up comedians like Richard Pryor, Chris Rock and Trevor Noah. However, they are black men, and Quentin Tarantino is white. I am not saying everyone who enjoys watching this movie without reservations is racist, nor that anyone who worked on *Pulp Fiction* or *Django Unchained* is a racist (well, except maybe Tarantino). Samuel L. Jackson, who was in both movies, stated that he didn't have any problems with Tarantino's constant use of the n-word, while Spike Lee has forcibly come out against what he thinks is Tarantino's overuse of the word in all his movies.[25]

I can't even count how many gory and haunting scenes are in the two movies. One of them, which I'm not going to describe, has stayed in my head for years.

I've also found that watching exceedingly violent films is just not healthy for me. I do still watch them occasionally if they are old favorites or ones I haven't seen before that I am excited to watch, but in general I just don't want these movies to stay in my head.

Overall Worst Offender: *Crocodile Dundee*

I first watched *Crocodile Dundee* in 1988. I was 7, and I watched it with a close friend and her family at a drive-in. (It was a double feature with *Twins*.) I remember loving the movie then. It's about Mick "Crocodile" Dundee, a wild man who lives his life outdoors in the Australian outback. Linda, a reporter, flies from her hometown of New York City to Australia to interview him about his experiences in the outback, and they spend some harrowing days exploring his stomping grounds. She then invites him

---

[25] Mottram 2013

to travel with her to New York. Once there, Mick realizes he doesn't belong in the city.

I've rewatched the movie over the years, and at some point there were at least two screwed-up moments that jumped out at me.

In one, a transgender woman is at a bar Mick has gone to, and he starts flirting with her. Several men in the bar tell him that the woman is "really" a man and they call her a gay slur. Mick decides to grab her genitals. He pronounces her a man, and everyone laughs. Later, he grabs another woman's genitals to see if she is "really" a man. The woman is surprised at first but then acts as if she enjoyed the experience. Mick's behavior is excused.

One of the things I didn't realize until I read the article "Crocodile Dundee was sexist, racist and homophobic. Let's not bring that back" by Luke Buckmaster of *The Guardian* was that Mick talks about the Australian aborigines (people who are native to the country) as if they were children. I also didn't realize until this most recent viewing how horribly sexist the movie is. Mick talks endlessly about how men are superior to women.[26] Also, the women in the movie constantly need Mick to save them from one thing or another.

---

[26] Buckmaster 2018

CHAPTER 10

How Watching Violent Movies Can Be Bad for Us

Washington University professor Jeff Zacks has explored how watching movies affects us emotionally. I was intrigued by this quote from a piece by Southern California Public Radio's Sanden Totten, concerning how people often react when watching *Rocky II*:

"'Just try not to flinch when you watch that… Basically, you are getting punched in the face on the screen.' Zacks says that flinch response is the result of hundreds of thousands of years of evolution. Our ancient ancestors developed reflexes to dodge incoming objects. So today, even though we know we're safe watching Rocky on the screen, we still might flinch involuntarily…"[27]

The piece also talked about a person who watched *The Hunger Games: Mockingjay, Part 1* and said that

---

[27] Totten 2014

the movie so disturbed her she was "still stressed out" after she finished watching the movie.

I am a huge fan of *The Hunger Games* series, both in movie and book form, but the whole series is about Katniss and her friends, family (and, really, just about everyone she knows) dealing with years or even decades of trauma, violence, and war. I am not surprised that the movie affected this woman so much.

Cinematherapists Gary Solomon and Birgit Wolz recommend several movies in their books that I consider excessively violent. In Solomon's *Reel Therapy: How Movies Inspire You to Overcome Life's Problems*, he claims that "There is no scientific proof or solid evidence"[28] that watching violent films affects people. Therefore, he doesn't have any compunction recommending extremely violent movies to his clients.

Since that book came out in 2001, forensic psychiatrists Vasilis K. Pozios, Praveen R. Kambam, and H. Eric Bender studied several meta-analyses concerning an association between real-world violence and violence in movies and other media. (A meta-analysis is a research method that combines the

[28] Solomon 2001

results of several related studies to produce better results.)

In their 2013 piece in the *New York Times*, "Does Media Violence Lead to the Real Thing?" they state that "[t]here is now consensus that exposure to media violence is linked to actual violent behavior—a link found by many scholars to be on par with the correlation of exposure to secondhand smoke and the risk of lung cancer."

Scientists who have studied the issue don't, however, state that watching movies directly causes someone to commit violent acts. Instead, they call it a "risk factor" for such future actions.[29] The authors state that they aren't calling for these types of movies to be banned. Instead, they believe that watching violence in movies is a risk factor that can be more easily addressed, as opposed to other ones that are difficult or even impossible to change, like the gender of the person committing the violence or how much the person or their family earns.

One other thing to keep in mind is that dozens of things are risk factors for future violence. Risk factors, by definition, don't cause anything to happen, but they can *possibly* increase the chances of something happening. You will obviously not commit assault only

---

[29] Pozios, Kambam, & Bender 2013

because you watched an actor pretend to beat someone up.

However, I agree with Solomon that you can still get a lot out of certain brutal movies. The first movie that came to mind when I started thinking about this was *The Color Purple*, a movie about a woman named Celie (played as an adult by Whoopi Goldberg) who has been subjected to a long period of incest (her father gets her pregnant twice when she is a young teen), sexual, physical, and emotional abuse. You also see Oprah Winfrey in her acting debut playing Sofia, a woman who is beaten nearly to death by the police after getting arrested. Some of these events occur off-screen and some on-screen.

Sounds horrific, right? However, watching such a movie could help those who have gone through or are currently going through such abuse to feel less alone and, if they blame themselves for this kind of abuse, they might see how it is not their fault in any way. They might even get out of an abusive relationship.

For those who haven't experienced or witnessed abuse by police officers, they will now see exactly how awful it is when law enforcement become extremely violent towards alleged offenders. There really is a tradeoff here.

Still, I think that certain movies have less of a tradeoff or none at all, including the movies discussed by David Wong of the website *Cracked.com*.

He wrote about the danger of watching certain violent movies, such as *Transformers*, in his insightful piece, "5 Ways You Don't Realize Movies Are Controlling Your Brain." He singled out *Transformers*, pointing to the fact that the movie's message is that violent conflict is cool and a joy to watch and gives the impression that brutal conflict has no repercussions. Wong believes that when it comes to all films, "the movie's 'agenda' is nothing more than a lot of creative people passing along their own psychological hang-ups, prejudices, superstitions, [and] ignorance" because they work on our minds like myths or stories. According to Wong, since the brain has evolved to think in stories, watching movies without realizing their potential effect on you can be dangerous.[30] I wholeheartedly agree with him.

That's why I was incredibly careful about the movies I chose for this book. I rewatched them and scrutinized them, looking for the ick factor. I want to show that while movies can strongly influence us, we can pick the best of the best to fill us with joy and empathy.

---

[30] Wong 2012

PART IV

Our Favorite Movies

Drumroll, please! You've finally arrived at the best part!

It's time to talk about the 12 movies I picked for you. Here are the sections included for each movie chapter:

Cast/Directed By/Writing Credits—the only things that I might need to explain here are what terms like "story by" and "additional story material by/additional dialogue by" mean. A "story by" credit means that the writer created or co-created the story—they came up with things like the plot and theme but didn't necessarily write the script itself. "Additional story material by" and "additional dialogue by" mean that the writer either contributed to previous drafts or provided additional written contributions to the final script. If you look closely, you might find that when there are multiple writers, sometimes their names are connected by "and" while sometimes "&" is used. This is because, according to the Writers Guild of America: "The word 'and' designates that the writers wrote separately and an ampersand ('&') denotes a writing team[31]."

Plot Summary—a brief description of the movie.

---

[31] https://www.wga.org/the-guild/about-us/faq#credits4

My Thoughts on This Movie—my takeaways from the movie. Things like what I loved about it, what I thought about certain characters and certain scenes, which characters I identified with, and how I felt about the themes.

How Watching This Movie Can Affect Our Mental Health—how it can lift my spirits, lessen anxiety and mania, help me to process things, make me feel less alone or less of a failure, and how it might also help you, dear reader.

Caveats and Triggers—caveats are things that I don't like about the movie, and triggers are things that happen in the movie that might cause the viewer to relive a traumatic event, like a depiction of physical abuse.

Fun Facts—these are interesting bits of information about the films, casts, and crews that I find marvelous.

I went around and around as to how I wanted to order the movies. Should they be ordered by how much I loved each one compared to the other movies? Should the order be according to how popular each movie is? Or when it came out?

What I decided to do first was divide the movies into these genres: dramedy (roughly equal parts drama and comedy), comedy (in its pure form), romantic comedy, and drama. Dramedies are my favorite because I am more apt to emotionally engage with the type of movie that has the potential for both laughter and tears, for absolute fear and absolute joy. Pure comedies and romantic comedies are next because they feel like coming home, but don't have as much of a range as dramedies. Dramas are last because they don't always give me to opportunity to giggle.

Within each category I grouped them from my first to least favorite (in some cases this was like trying to choose which of my children was my least favorite. Except I don't have children. But you know what I mean.)

Okay, let's go!

CHAPTER 11

Inside Out
(2015)

CAST:

Amy Poehler—Joy

Phyllis Smith—Sadness

Bill Hader—Fear

Lewis Black—Anger

Mindy Kaling—Disgust

Richard Kind—Bing Bong

Kaitlyn Dias—Riley

DIRECTED BY:

Pete Docter and Ronnie Del Carmen

WRITING CREDITS:

Screenplay by: Pete Docter, Meg LeFauve & Josh Cooley

Original Story by: Pete Docter & Ronnie Del Carmen

Additional story material by: Michael Arndt & Simon Rich

Additional dialogue by: Bill Hader & Amy Poehler

Plot Summary

In this animated movie, an 11-year-old girl, Riley, must move from her beloved Minnesota home to San Francisco because her father got a new job there. She has a tough time with the new place from the get-go. She misses her friends, her ice hockey team, her old house, and pretty much everything about Minnesota. Her emotions are depicted as characters—Joy, Sadness, Anger, Disgust, and Fear—and they become so messed up after the move that Sadness and Joy get lost in Riley's mind. The two emotions go on a journey to get back to emotional headquarters, so Riley can feel Joy and Sadness again.

My Thoughts on This Movie

There's a reason why I dressed up as Sadness for Halloween 2016. I even applied blue makeup to my face, neck and hands, and used blue hairspray, because I commit! (Man, it was tough to get the makeup off and the hairspray completely washed out of my hair. I had to do some crowdsourcing to figure out how to de-blue myself.)

The character of Sadness makes me so happy. It may sound strange to hear that, but it's true. I don't know if I've ever identified more with a character. She's overweight, wears glasses, and is shy and awkward. She doesn't have control over how she feels and sometimes how she acts. She cares deeply about others—especially Joy. She feels a lot of shame. She's a true friend. She also enjoys being sad at times—she loves watching a film where a pet dies. (Not in a weird way though. I couldn't think of any other way to word that sentence without it seeming like she may be some kind of monster. She just enjoys being sad and crying sometimes). She also likes it when Riley gets wet and cold when it rains.

Bing Bong was Riley's imaginary friend when she was little, and when he meets up with Joy and Sadness, he does his best to help them on their journey. There are two scenes with Bing Bong that I love; at least one of them will make me cry every time I watch the movie.

I didn't cry at movies, or in life that much, for a long time. There was something blocked emotionally. I suddenly realized about 15 years ago that I was tearing up way more often than I had before when watching certain movies. At first I felt that I had just become weak, but then I realized that I could connect with the characters on a deeper level if I let myself cry, and that crying doesn't make you weak. I agree with cinematherapist Birgit Wolz about how she feels that crying while seeing a film is cathartic. Just like Sadness, we all need to cry sometimes, and watching a movie that has sadness in it is a perfect time to do so.

In the first of the two scenes that will make me cry, Bing Bong is feeling depressed because his rocket ship/wagon (something that is incredibly important to him) was sent to the memory dump—where memories go to die. He thinks that not only can he no longer take Riley on adventures, but that she will completely forget him. Sadness helps him keep going on their journey by empathizing with his sorrow. This is my favorite scene in the whole movie.

Spoiler alert! The second scene that can make me bawl is when Bing Bong saves Joy. He does this knowing that he might not survive. He feels it is more important for Riley to have Joy in her life than to have him in her life.

My favorite Riley scene is where she and her parents are all hugging each other, and she is crying while smiling. It's so good to have those moments: sad at one circumstance (it's hard to move to a new place), but happy with another (how much her parents love and support her). Part of growing up is having more complex emotions and memories.

There are also some hilarious moments in this movie—it wouldn't be so enjoyable if it was all tough stuff. Phyllis Smith manages to steal the movie as

Sadness. It takes a truly remarkable actor who can make a blue character so funny. Of course, part of her humor comes from the writers, a truly impressive bunch that includes the gifted Bill Hader and Amy Poehler (pulling double duty here with their voice work as Fear and Joy, respectively).

You may nearly wet yourself from laughing when the movie goes inside some other people's minds. Riley's mom's mind is an interesting place, full of fantasies of a certain helicopter pilot she used to date. Interestingly, her mom's emotion of sadness is the leader in her emotional headquarters. It seems that her deep empathy for her daughter comes from this emotion, just like how Riley's empathy comes from Sadness. Riley's dad enjoys replaying old hockey games in his head (which can get him into trouble), and his emotional leader is anger.

How Watching This Movie Can Affect Our Mental Health

I think watching this movie can help everyone feel better about uncomfortable emotions because the main theme is how natural they all are. You can't banish an emotion from yourself. You can't rein them in all the time. You may think that you have, but they are still there, waiting. Whatever you may be doing to hide from them—things like working all the time, exercising excessively, overeating or using substances to numb yourself—they will still bubble up.

You are not a bad person if you feel anger. When I was growing up, anger was the worst emotion to express in my family. You weren't supposed to raise your voice, let alone yell. You either worked out conflict by calmly talking about the situation or just passively dealing with it internally. I won't even get into the gendered ideas around who is "allowed" to express anger. The good thing, though, is that I am skilled at staying calm or walking away from a situation where I know I might spew some stupidly angry words. Notice that I said skilled and not perfect.

Remember how I was talking about Wolz's concept of the shadow self, the part of ourselves that we don't want to even think about? I would wager that every person who watches this movie feels that at least one of the emotions is part of their shadow self. Mine is anger. If you're wondering what yours is, figure out what your least favorite character is of the five emotions, and I'll bet you a pretty penny that's the winner.

You can try to be happy all the time and to push your kids or others to do so, but it will backfire. Part of the reason Riley starts thinking about running away and gets so mad at her parents is that her mom pushes her to act happy. Riley is also mad because she feels her parents, especially her dad, aren't listening to her.

Finally, I relate to Riley because I was 14 when my family moved from Wisconsin to Colorado. I have always had a tough time making friends and I had finally found my awesomely unique friends about two years before we left. I didn't adjust well for a time and I felt a lot of anger that we had to move. You hear about how resilient kids are, how they can adjust quickly to new scenery. In reality, it's a common experience for kids to go through a really tough time after a move. It's okay for everyone to be angry, sad, fearful, or disgusted when they move somewhere new.

Caveats and Triggers

Nada.

Fun Facts

Sadness wasn't only *my* favorite emotion. She was considered the breakout character, which really surprised Phyllis Smith, who voiced Sadness. In a 2015 interview with *Entertainment Weekly*'s Nina Terrero, Smith talked about how one time when she was shopping at a Target in her hometown, a 6-year-old girl recognized her voice and came up to her. The girl asked Smith to sign her Sadness doll. That story makes me think about how that girl might be more able to deal with her own feelings of sadness as she grows up because of how much she loves the character.

Smith's first career was as a professional dancer. This included time as an NFL cheerleader and as a burlesque dancer. After an injury forced her to quit dancing, she spent 19 years as a casting agent and then started acting in 2005 at the age of 53. Yet another reason to love this woman: when she was asked by Terrero about whether she might ever write a memoir, she dismissed it, saying, "I've never thought of it. Someone recently told me, 'Phyllis, you should write a book' and I said, 'Really?' I'm just a weird, normal person.'"[32] I love the idea that someone could be weird and normal at the same time.

The script and story went through many permutations over the years the Pixar team worked on the movie. In earlier versions of the story, instead of Sadness, Joy was paired with Bing Bong or Fear throughout the movie. Joy was sometimes aggressive or mean. There was a Tragic Vampire Romance Island in Riley's head in one version.

The movie won an Oscar for Best Animated Feature Film and Co-director and co-writer Pete Docter accepted the Oscar and gave a moving speech. He encouraged kids struggling with difficult emotions to understand that everyone their age will do so and find ways to engage in creativity to help

---

[32] Terrero 2015

them find ways to help improve their moods. The movie also won a Golden Globe and 93 other awards.

Docter had the inspiration for the final script as he watched his daughter, Elie, start to increasingly display emotions like sadness and disgust when she was 11. Elie was the voice for the young Ellie character in *Up*, which was also co-directed and co-written by Docter. In one of the Blu-Ray special features, Elie and her best friend Gracie Giacchino (daughter of the movie's composer Michael Giacchino) filmed a short documentary about their dads' experiences working on the movie.

Outside of Riley's family, we get to see inside more humans' minds—and a few animals'. Peering inside Riley's teacher's mind, we find out that the frustrated teacher calms herself by thinking about her boyfriend, the same helicopter pilot that Riley's mom went out with and often fantasizes about. We observe the emotions inside a boy's mind meltdown when he accidentally bumps into Riley—and the boy enjoys an emotional jam fest in another special feature. We also peek inside the mind of a birthday clown, a classmate of Riley's, a restaurant worker, a dog, and a cat (my favorite!).

CHAPTER 12

Eternal Sunshine of the Spotless Mind (2004)

CAST:

Jim Carrey—Joel Barish

Kate Winslet—Clementine Kruczynski

Kirsten Dunst—Mary

Mark Ruffalo—Stan

Elijah Wood—Patrick

Tom Wilkinson—Dr. Mierzwiak

DIRECTED BY:

Michel Gondry

WRITING CREDITS:

Screenplay by: Charlie Kaufman

Story by: Charlie Kaufman, Michel Gondry & Pierre Bismuth

Plot Summary

Joel and Clementine have a sometimes lovely, sometimes trying, romantic relationship. After a grueling fight, which included some incredibly hurtful words from Joel, Clementine decides to literally erase Joel from her memories by undergoing a procedure done by the Lacuna Corporation, a company that specializes in purging people's memories. Out of anger, Joel decides to do the same.

The staff at Lacuna include Stan, who tries desperately to finish the job of Joel's erasure and is deeply in love with Mary; Mary, who is fond of quotes and secretly in love with Dr. Mierzwiak; Dr. Mierzwiak, who is the head of Lacuna, has a secret of his own and tries his best to help all his clients leave their pain behind; and creepy Patrick, who falls in love with Clementine while he is helping erase her memories of Joel. Dr. Mierzwiak and his team have a lot of problems with Joel, who fights losing his memories of Clementine while the team works hard to erase everything that has to do with Clementine.

My Thoughts on This Movie

If you could erase the memories of a romantic relationship, would you? What if the other person erased their memories of you? Would you do it out of anger? What if it was wonderful at times but deeply difficult at other times? I've asked people if they would delete these types of memories, and they overwhelmingly said no. I'm not talking about abusive relationships here, to be clear. I didn't ask specifically about relationships that were abusive—I could see how that type of erasure could, in some cases, be beneficial.

Spoiler alert! Even with both Joel and Clementine going through this process, there still is something that holds the two together. Fate? Feelings that can't be erased? Something else? The movie leaves that up to the viewer to decide.

I would not willingly obliterate any memories of past relationships. I would not willingly delete any recollections that I have, period. I believe they *all* help make me who I am, for better or for worse. I believe that one of the reasons we are here on earth is to learn things, and you can't do that as effectively by purposefully ridding yourself of memories.

Here's the thing—losing memories doesn't necessarily mean erasing feelings, as you will see in the movie. There are things deep down inside you that may never go away. They may lessen, you may be able to find ways to work through emotions, but that doesn't mean the feelings are gone.

One of the things the movie examines is how a person reacts when they are hurt and angry. Clementine felt so much pain hearing Joel demean her during an emotionally charged fight, she believed that the only way to fully deal with the situation was to erase her memories of Joel. Once Joel found out what she had done he was so hurt and angry that he did the same. It can seem very satisfying to make split-second decisions because of negative feelings. Yet it is so important that we try to think over things before we act out when we experience an intensely negative emotion.

One of the fun things about this movie—and it was very much touted during its theatrical release—was that Jim Carrey (Joel) plays a Kate Winslet-type character, while Winslet, as Clementine, plays more of a Jim Carrey-like person. Carrey in this role is quiet, introspective, and anxious. Winslet is boisterous, free-spirited, and friendly. Carrey still has fun with the part—my favorite scenes are of the former couple frolicking together.

I really identify with both Joel and Clementine. Together, they are the two sides of my personality. At times, I too can be quiet, introspective, and anxious, like Joel. This represents my introverted side and my diagnosis of generalized anxiety disorder. I also have the gift of introspection, which is mostly good as I can observe what is going on with my mental health and find ways to right the ship when I am heading for a psychiatric episode.

As for my Clementine side, though I am not an extrovert, I do consider myself to be an ambivert (someone who can access both their introvert and extrovert sides). I love being friendly, especially when doing so leads to deep conversations with people. I can also be very lively at times, depending on the circumstance. I am in so many ways a free spirit.

Like Clementine, I am an incredibly independent person and always have been. I could never be in a romantic relationship where the other person is my "better half" and we spend all our time together. I also don't put on masks. What you see is what you get.

How Watching This Movie Can Affect Our Mental Health

Let's try the other side of erasing memories: what if you wanted to keep the recollections you lost? I've had to deal with both short-term and long-term memory loss for nearly 20 years. This loss is due to both my mental health symptoms and the psychiatric medications I use to treat them (though of course the passage of time takes a toll). They have wreaked havoc on my brain. There are many things I would like to remember but can't. Sometimes I feel cheated because of this.

Whether it is the semi-frequent inability to hold in my head the whole thread of a conversation or to remember more of the wonderful moments of spending time with my Grandma Feustel, I can get despondent because of my memory holes. There are years of my life that I do not remember at all, including some during my 20s.

For me, having short-term memory issues makes me feel stupid, and I worry that I may appear dim to others when my issues are apparent. Some questions I've often had to ask myself: Did I just miss the turn to my friend's house, the place I've been to 20 times? (Answer: Yes, yes, I did. Thank goodness for GPS when I'm lost.) Did I wash my face at the end of my shower? (Hmmmm. Maybe? I think so?) What's the name of that friend that I've talked with at parties at least six times? (I'll usually figure out the name, either by asking someone else or looking at a Facebook event page to figure it out. In the meantime, I feel anxious about it.)

I know no one's memory is perfect. I know that we will naturally lose memories over time. I know that there are people who have it worse than I do. It's still demoralizing and can make me feel stupid.

How about you? Have you lost a lot of memories that were important to you, or do you suffer from memory issues? Do you feel the frustration and pain that can come from the same kind of experiences I've had? I'm not just talking about those with mental health issues. Everyone can experience these situations.

You might also have a friend or relative who has moderate to severe memory problems. I would encourage you to be patient with them and talk about all the good times you have had together. Think about how it probably has been at least somewhat scary or depressing for them to lose part of themselves, just like how Joel (or at least his psyche) experiences fear and sadness as Clementine is being stripped from his memories.

Caveats and Triggers

Patrick is very creepy and could be considered a stalker. He steals Clementine's underwear and purposely takes things of hers or Joel's that showed how much they loved each other. By using or referencing these things, he tries to make Clementine fall in love with him.

Fun Facts

A delightfully nerdy website called *Adam Savage's Tested* has a piece by Jody Duncan and Joe Fordham about how the director, Michel Gondry, was able to create such a unique movie:

"The surreal images in *Eternal Sunshine of the Spotless Mind*—digital effects sprinkled with in-camera and forced perspective gags, all achieved without the use of bluescreen or motion control—sprang from a filmmaker who approaches visual effects more as a magician than a technician. 'A magician makes you look at one place while the trick is happening somewhere else,' said [visual effects supervisor Louis] Morin. 'Michel does that with effects. You expect an effect at one point in a shot, but the effect is already done by the time you get there. He fools you—and that's part of his cleverness. Everything is possible in his mind.'"[33]

One of my favorite anecdotes about the movie is this: In one scene, in which you see "two" Joels, Carrey played both Joels by running back and forth behind the camera while quickly doing his own wardrobe change. What feels like a special effect because it doesn't seem possible in real life, is in fact more trickery.

If you are curious to know more about the effects, I recommend reading The A.V. Club's piece "Here's

---

how special effects were made for Eternal Sunshine of the Spotless Mind." [34]

The movie won best original screenplay at the Oscars, and the director Michel Gondry, Pierre Bismuth, and screenwriter Charlie Kaufman collected trophies for their writing credits. Kaufman has written several delightfully weird movies including *Being John Malkovich,* which also spends a lot of time inside of a character's mind.

[34] Henne 2015

CHAPTER 13

Fried Green Tomatoes (1991)

CAST:

Kathy Bates—Evelyn Couch

Mary Stuart Masterson—Idgie Threadgoode

Mary-Louise Parker—Ruth Jamison

Jessica Tandy—Ninny Threadgoode

DIRECTED BY:

Jon Avnet

WRITING CREDITS:

Screenplay by: Fannie Flagg and Carol
Sobieski

Based on the novel *Fried Green
Tomatoes at the Whistle Stop Cafe* by:
Fannie Flagg

Plot Summary

Evelyn Couch (who lives in the 1980s) is a deeply unhappy housewife who uses food to self-medicate. She meets wise Ninny Threadgoode when she is visiting a relative at a nursing home. Ninny tells her the story of Idgie Threadgoode and Ruth Jamison, two women from the 1920s who became very close. Idgie, with the help of family and friends, rescued a pregnant Ruth from her abusive husband and took her in. Idgie and Ruth were nearly inseparable and started a café together. Evelyn gets caught up in the story while forming a close bond with Ninny, which inspires Evelyn to improve her life.

My Thoughts on This Movie

I clearly remember that during past viewings, I thought that Idgie was romantically interested in Ruth, but the feelings were one-sided. When I rewatched it recently, I thought it was possible that they were involved in a romantic relationship. Interestingly, cinematherapist Brigit Wolz's online piece on this movie states that they were a couple.[35]

During a courtroom scene in the movie, when asked why she left her husband to live with Idgie, Ruth

---

[35] Wolz 2018

stated that Idgie was her best friend. You can take that statement at face value—but in the 1920s, Ruth obviously couldn't say in public that they were romantically involved.

For me, there is one scene that convinced me as a child watching it that Idgie was in love with Ruth. Idgie had just gotten Ruth drunk and they are playing poker by a lake. The way that Idgie looks at Ruth in that scene told me that she must be in love with her.

This is another reason to love this movie—the ambiguity. How many movies are there where you can have vastly different ideas about the main characters and their relationship with each other? Through my informal polling, everyone I talked to thought that Idgie was attracted to Ruth, but not all of them thought Ruth felt the same way.

Since I am almost always averse to wearing anything that would be considered overly feminine, I felt a deep kinship with and admiration of Idgie. She never wears anything but the male clothes of the period unless she is forced to. When I wear skirts and dresses (which is very rare) I call it my "girl drag." My favorite outfit is a t-shirt and sweatpants, which I would wear 24/7 if I could.

Ever since I saw the movie the first time, I wanted to be fierce like Idgie so that I could be brave and able to be myself. I am more like Evelyn, who has overeating problems and is depressed. She is also timid and shy, which I can be depending on the situation. She trusts easily and blames herself for what other people do to her. She's very childlike and immediately gets swept up in Ninny and her story.

As the movie goes on, I'm torn about Evelyn. I'm glad she becomes more assertive and feels empowered and happier, but she can be very aggressive at times. She seems to sometimes go too far in the other direction.

How Watching This Movie Can Affect Our Mental Health

As I said earlier, I relate to Evelyn in both being overweight and being timid (at least some of the time). I think that this movie shows that it's preferable not to be timid. (But try not to go too far in the other direction!)

One thing that I am not timid about is my reaction to people expressing disdain or dismissal of mental health issues. In fact, like Evelyn in the second half of the movie, I get assertive. I must admit, I may even come across as a little scary.

What I most want to do with my life is help stamp out stigma against those who struggle with such problems. I was at a party about two years ago when I got into a heated discussion with a man about mental health issues. He believed that often teenagers pretend they have mental health issues because they think it makes them cool.

I became livid. I told him off for a good five minutes. The worst part of it? He works with teenagers. Here's the thing. I don't personally know the kids he works with. Is there a possibility that they are not, in fact, diagnosed with mental health issues? Sure.

However, if they are not, it's likely they are looking for attention, for someone to see them. So, by either not believing the kids or by not paying attention to them, he's not doing his job.

Do you feel like a doormat sometimes? Do you find that people walk all over you and you fear standing up for yourself? If you feel that way that doesn't mean there's anything wrong with you. Please don't go into a shame spiral like I have so many times. You are not weak or broken, or anything like that. You have your reasons for being so timid and maybe, like me, it was just the way for you to survive whatever problems you had.

I will tell you that it's okay for you to be assertive. It doesn't matter what gender you are or what people expect of you. It matters that you stick to your own personal values and speak your truth. Keep in mind we are all human. You don't have to be assertive all the time or turn aggressive or passive-aggressive. I encourage you to pick your battles while staying true to who you are.

Caveats and Triggers:

I have no caveats, but there are some enormous potential triggers in this movie. If you are triggered by domestic violence or the physical and psychological violence that KKK members (or racists in general) wreak on those they hate, then be forewarned. This violence, since it is such a small part of the movie, doesn't register on my ick factor meter.

Fun Facts

In the book the movie is based on, *Fried Green Tomatoes at the Whistle Stop Café*, author Fannie Flag depicts Idgie and Ruth's relationship as a romantic one. The studio decided they should be in a platonic relationship instead. Director Jon Avnet obviously didn't completely let go of the idea that there was at least a one-sided romantic relationship. Need some proof? He felt that the food fight scene was a stand-in for a love scene.[36]

Speaking of that scene, when it came to creating it, each actress got to pick which food she would use as

---

[36] IMDB 2018

ammunition. They were then allowed to just go at it as the scene was completely improvised. It was all done in one take.

I find it incredibly interesting that though on the surface they were depicted as friends, some of the romantic relationship (or at least one-sided on Idgie's part) bled through enough that Brigit Wolz and I felt that there was something different going on. In the pieces and interviews I've seen online, there seems to be a consensus that Idgie and Ruth had a romantic relationship, with Malinda Lo of the website *After Ellen* calling it a "lesbian classic."[37] GLAAD, a U.S. non-governmental media monitoring organization founded by a group of LGBTQ+ writers and journalists, gave it their Media Award for Outstanding Film in 1992, due to the perceived nature of the relationship of Idgie and Ruth.

---

[37] Lo 2008

CHAPTER 14

A League of Their Own (1992)

CAST:

Geena Davis—Dottie Hinson

Lori Petty—Kit Keller

Tom Hanks—Jimmy Dugan

Madonna—Mae Mordabito

Rosie O'Donnell—Doris Murphy

Megan Cavanagh—Marla Hooch

DIRECTED BY:

Penny Marshall

WRITING CREDITS:

Screenplay by: Lowell Ganz & Babaloo Mandel

Story by: Kim Wilson & Kelly Candaele

Plot Summary

In real life, during WWII, with hundreds of professional baseball players fighting overseas including many of the best players of that period, Major League Baseball became a shadow of what it once was. People were worried the 1943 season would be completely canceled. Several prominent business people decided to fill the recreational void by creating the All-American Girls Professional Baseball League (AAGPBL) in 1943.

The rest of the story is loosely based on actual events.

Sisters Kit and Dottie, who have a stormy relationship, try out for the league and get placed on the Rockford Peaches team. Jimmy Dugan, their manager, has serious alcohol addiction issues and doesn't seem to give a crap about the league, other than getting a paycheck. The Peaches become a dynamic sisterhood with high-quality players who help to make the league more and more popular and fun during the 1943 season. The movie starts and ends with Dottie, Kit, and other surviving members of the AAGPBL in their 70s, exploring a brand-new exhibit at the National Baseball Hall of Fame featuring their league.

My Thoughts on This Movie

At the beginning of the movie, a talent scout for the league travels to Willamette, Oregon, to watch Kit and Dottie play in their hometown. He visits their farm and says that he only wants to recruit Dottie for tryouts, and she turns him down. When Kit begs the scout to take her with him, he agrees—but only if Dottie will come too. Kit then must plead with her sister to come, and finally succeeds. The two of them head with the scout to Chicago.

The core of this movie is about the difficult sisterly relationship between Kit and Dottie. They struggle to both love and like each other. For most of the movie, Kit is thought of as less than her sister by nearly everyone who knows the two of them—less beautiful, less talented at baseball, less logical, and less sweet. (I think Dottie is a classic beauty and Kit is more average looking. Dottie seems, at least most of the time, more talented than her sister.) Even Kit feels that Dottie is the better player.

Kit resents these types of criticisms, and the fact that the scout would only take her if her sister would go too rankles her. Dottie can sometimes give her sister a tough time, but it seems like Dottie doesn't believe that her sister is inferior to her. It's hard to tell as Dottie keeps nearly everything very close to the vest.

The sisters have fights, though Kit usually gets very emotional and angry, while Dottie usually stays cool and unflappable. At one point in the movie, after a giant fight, Dottie asks to be transferred to another team so they can have some distance, but things blow up in her face when instead Kit is transferred to another team. The sisterly relationship continues to deteriorate.

I relate to Kit and I see a lot of Dottie in my sister. I can be more emotional, with some serious mood swings at times. Jane's much better at keeping a cool head than I am. She has a knack for bringing people together, a trait that Dottie seems to have. She's also a very beautiful woman, not just in my eyes but in the eyes of others. I've felt jealous of her off and on over the years, just as Kit is jealous of Dottie.

The other character I identify with is Marla, who is a fellow Coloradoan, hailing from Fort Collins. On the way to tryouts, the sisters and the scout make a stop to check her out. We first see her uncanny hitting ability in wide and medium shots, but it's not until she comes forward shyly to talk to the scout that we see her close up. It's clear that her face is plain and she doesn't have a figure that was prized at the time (or now).

She's dismissed by the scout as he (like others) thinks that looks are just as important (if not more so) than talent in the new league. Dottie and Kit stand up for her and won't leave without her. This makes my heart glad. Marla ends up on the Peaches as well. Throughout the scenes she is in, she is sometimes belittled or ignored because of her looks. I have been dismissed like this myself.

One of the things I like most about the movie is that all the major characters and most of the minor ones are complex. Dottie can be unfeeling. Kit is passionate in both positive and negative ways. Jimmy (the manager) can be a jerk whether or not he's sober. He does have his moments and is an excellent manager when he "steps up to the plate." I think he would have been the villain or the antihero in any other movie, but I don't think I could categorize him as a hero, villain, or antihero here. He is simply a flawed man.

Even though now he's thought of more as a dramatic actor, Hanks almost exclusively acted in comedies and comedy-dramas like this movie for the first 12 years of his career. It's rare to have an actor who is at home in every type of genre he's ever been in. His physical comedy here is impeccable. If you want to see Hanks at the height of his physical comedy chops, check out *Joe Versus the Volcano* (see Chapter 20).

How Watching This Movie Can Affect Our Mental Health

It makes me feel a little less alone when I see this type of movie about sisters. Sometimes I get envious of sisters who have always been super close. It helps me to know that there isn't something wrong with my relationship with my sister. Even though we are very different people in several ways, we still love each other and can support each other through our struggles. We also never fought like the sisters did in this movie.

In the '90s part of the movie, you see that things have calmed down now that the sisters are in their 70s, but they still aren't especially close; they see each other only occasionally. I got the impression that throughout their lives they were better at experiencing brief, intense periods of love for each other, but not long-term devotion.

Here's my takeaway: you can love your sister even when relations are strained or when personality or other types of differences get in the way. It's okay to be an emotional person but be aware of how your behavior will impact the people around you. It's okay not to be the conventionally beautiful one.

If you also have a sibling (or siblings), did you sometimes have a turbulent relationship with them? For only children, you might have had relationships with parents, extended family members or friends that make the relationship between Dottie and Kit feel familiar. Whatever type of difficult relationship it was, I encourage you to watch this movie and write about any feelings or thoughts that spring up regarding your family or friends. You could even write a note to them about how you feel. You don't need to share it with them if you don't want to. If you do, you could send an email, a text, or even that old-timey thing called a "letter." I know from experience that journaling has helped me deal with any difficult feelings and baggage around various ties I have to people.

I very much relate to Marla's struggles of being belittled or ignored because of her appearance. It didn't matter how smart or funny I was—I was big and not a pretty princess. I, like Marla, prefer to wear unisex clothes 99% of the time. Unlike Marla, I have never been forced to wear a dress, and a mini dress at that, like the uniforms that the players had to wear.

Do you always wear clothes that are "traditionally" more masculine or more feminine, and this goes against what mainstream society or those around you think you "should" wear? Were you ever forced to wear certain types of clothing that you didn't want to? I can only imagine the discomfort and anger you probably felt.

Do people make fun of you or ignore you because of how you look? If so, I will send you virtual hugs or give you real-life ones if I meet you in person. This is a crappy thing to go through. You are not alone; your worth is not based on your appearance—screw those people.

Caveats and Triggers

I'm troubled both by some of Jimmy's actions and how they are played for laughs. He can be a mean drunk and insults several women on the team and makes one cry. Black-out drunk, he kisses a woman when she wasn't expecting a kiss, and then realizes what he's done and freaks out because he thought she was someone else. He also slaps her on the butt and throws a baseball mitt at a kid's head so hard the kid becomes dizzy and falls over. The only good thing is that this kind of behavior makes up a very small percentage of the movie. As I said before, his physical comedy is impeccable, so I might automatically laugh at some of these scenes and then feel rather bad about it.

Fun Facts

Like Fried Green Tomatoes (see Chapter 13), there's some ambiguity to this movie. Not every viewer agrees on how exactly the ending went down. I won't say much if you haven't seen the movie, other than this question: does Dottie make a big mistake, or does she purposely do something to help her sister?

In my informal polling, people who have seen the movie overwhelmingly believe that Dottie is helping Kit at the end. There's a lot of debate online, by both professional and amateur writers, that it happened, it didn't, or there is no way to know. I personally think that Dottie was trying to help her sister. Why? I think she did it because she wanted to give her sister a gift. Dottie knew that Kit felt she was always in Dottie's shadow, and that she wanted to help her sister stop feeling this way without it being obvious. Dottie wanted to repair their fractured relationship and thought this would be a way to help.

In real life, it was gum mogul and Chicago Cubs owner Philip K. Wrigley who was the brainchild behind the league, not the fictional man in the movie, candy-maker Walter Harvey. I'm not exactly sure why they decided to go with the Harvey character. The Wrigley family didn't like the idea of the movie, so they wouldn't give permission to use the Wrigley name? Chocolate is a million times better than gum? Who knows?

Historical Fun Facts

The league played from 1943-1954, "with attendance peaking in the late 1940s at 910,000 fans. But the league's decentralization, a dearth of qualified players and the rise of televised major league games eventually led to its demise, with players retiring their gloves after the close of the 1954 season."[38]

Dottie's character was based on Dorothy "Dottie" Damenshek, who was considered the best female professional in the league and played from 1943-1953. She was given the chance to play on a men's minor league team, but turned it down as, according to her, "I thought it was a publicity stunt..."[39]

---

[38] Berman 2015
[39] Williams 2010

CHAPTER 15

Defending Your Life (1991)

CAST:

Albert Brooks—Daniel

Meryl Streep—Julia

Rip Torn—Bob Diamond

Lee Grant—Lena Foster

DIRECTED BY:

Albert Brooks

WRITING CREDITS:

Screenplay by: Albert Brooks

Plot Summary

Alone on his birthday, Daniel buys a BMW, and during a ride around L.A., accidentally drives into a bus and is killed. He ends up in the afterlife, in a place called Judgment City, where everyone must go on trial to determine whether they will be reincarnated as another person on earth or move on to some higher plane of existence.

If it is determined that a person lived life out of fear, they are reincarnated. If they lived free of fear, they go on. While Daniel's trial is not going so well, his bright spot is an effortless romance with Julia, a woman who is clearly fearless and will move on. He must decide if he is capable of being daring during his time with Julia, thus possibly continuing their relationship on the next level.

My Thoughts on This Movie

Albert Brooks based the plot loosely on eastern religions that have reincarnation as part of their dogma, with the idea that human beings will eventually move on to another spiritual plane. Of any afterlife I've seen depicted in a fictional universe, this movie comes the closest to my beliefs about reincarnation. I don't think I will go on trial, but I believe that a) this is not my first lifetime and b) there will be some kind of decision made after I die as to whether I will be sent back to earth or go on. Who are the beings that would make the determination? What would they be like? I don't know, but I don't think they would be as judgmental as most of those who work in Judgment City.

Daniel is represented by Bob Diamond, and his prosecutor is Lena Foster, aka "The Dragon Lady." Diamond, for all his smarts, seems ineffectual, while The Dragon Lady is talented. Every trial has a set number of days from a person's life that the prosecution can bring up. With each day, The Dragon Lady brings up fearful memory after fearful memory. Daniel doesn't fight back against a schoolyard bully, he doesn't push for a raise, he doesn't invest in a startup company that would have made him a millionaire, he freaks out before a big presentation, and more.

I started thinking about whether The Dragon Lady could metaphorically be a self-critical inner voice. That voice that says things like: "You should have stuck up for yourself. Why can't you just have some self-respect? There's something wrong with you if you can't do this." It's the voice that reminds us when we are at our lowest about all the ways we've screwed up. Also, in Daniel's case, perhaps the voice also meanly said, "Be a man."

I find the romance between Daniel and Julia both original and refreshingly complex. They meet at a comedy show. The comedian, a citizen of the city, is bombing, and Daniel starts heckling him. Julia notices Daniel and comes over, thinking she knows him from somewhere, though they have never met. (I wonder if they had known each other in a former life. That would have been so cool!)

At first, they seem like a strange pair. He's a worrier and a pessimist; she's carefree, fearless, and an optimist. But they can make each other laugh, she brings out a kinder side in him, and he can relax with her. In her most recent lifetime, Julia had adopted a child, saved her family (including her cat) from their burning house when it caught on fire, and seemingly never gave in to fear. Clearly, she will be moving on rather than reincarnating. (As far as I'm concerned, she gets extra points for being a cat person.) Daniel, with all his imperfections, will need a miracle to keep from returning to earth.

I love the Julia character so much. Her favorite part of Judgment City? The fact that everyone can eat as much as they want and not gain weight. That would be my favorite too (well, and the Past Lives Pavilion— more on that later). She's also super silly. There's a great scene where Daniel and Julia are eating dinner, and her pasta noodle is seemingly endless. She keeps slurping and slurping it, with Daniel begging her to just bite it. She finally slurps it up, grins, and gives a big thumbs-up.

It's also very entertaining to watch a woman who is thought of as a fantastic dramatic actress have so much fun with this part. Over the course of her career, Meryl Streep has had a fair number of fantastic comedic or part comedic/part dramatic roles, like *Death Becomes Her*, *The Devil Wears Prada* and *Julie & Julia*.

Defending Your Life came out in 1991, and I first watched it a year or two later, at age 11 or 12. It made a huge impression on me, and I am not alone. When I was talking about including this movie in my book during a family reunion, one of my cousins said that she had seen it in the theaters when she was 8 and it also made a sizable impression on her. Another cousin told me that that he had seen it on TV sometime in his mid-teens and could recall that it had really affected him.

How Watching This Movie Can Affect Our Mental Health

Do you hear The Dragon Lady's voice in your ear? The voice that reminds you of all your mistakes, fears and anxieties? I know I do, especially when I can't sleep.

We play things in our minds over and over. The Dragon Lady can haunt us for most of our lives to one degree or another. These Dragon Lady memories of humiliations, regrettable actions or inactions may stay with us for decades. I remember many specific instances of being bullied at school for being fat or just plain weird. I remember the times when I've treated family or friends badly.

No one is perfect, though many of us wish with all our hearts we could be. If you are constantly playing these things out in your mind, I want you to know you're not alone in feeling this way. Also, from my personal experience and through talking with other people with anxiety issues, I know that we can sometimes believe that because of the way we have behaved people have judged us harshly and perhaps don't want to be friendly anymore. The truth is, that usually isn't the case. Others may have either forgotten what happened entirely (at least if it was a while ago), weren't affected by our actions at all, or will never be as hard on us as we are on ourselves.

I've found that if I think I have wronged someone, the best way to go is to bring it out in the open and apologize and see what happens. Usually, the person either thinks it wasn't a big deal, or they accept the apology and we can move on. Of course, some of the people we think we have wronged may be deceased or out of our lives, or there may be a legitimate reason why talking to the person about this is a bad idea. In these instances, talking it through with a compassionate person can be helpful.

Not only do we have to deal at least occasionally with the Dragon Lady, but sometimes she sets off a shame spiral. What do I mean? Let me explain with the following example.

I start by thinking about a past humiliation caused by a bully, and I tell myself that it is shameful that I still feel that humiliation and anxiety. I tell myself I should just get over it. "Why dwell on the past? You're wasting your life doing that. Just get over it!"

Now I'm anxious that I am dwelling on the past when I "shouldn't be" and I feel there's something wrong with me because of how I'm feeling. Then, as if to torture myself, I start to think of another bully/humiliation memory, feel anxious when I "shouldn't be" and feel there's even more wrong with me.

These thoughts and feelings can become an endless feedback loop of self-shaming.

Shaming doesn't ever help anxiety. Indeed, shaming people, in general, is rarely the way to go to change their behavior for the better. Shaming people who are against vaccinating their children isn't likely to get them to change their minds. Shaming people of a different belief system than yours probably will not win you converts. Scientific fact: shaming people who are overweight can lead to them gaining weight.

Shaming yourself for, say, playing tens of thousands (maybe even hundreds of thousands) of games of Spider Solitaire on various devices over the last 20 years won't stop you for good, even if playing sometimes aggravates your old wrist or shoulder injuries and is a complete waste of time.

What can help stop shame spirals and The Dragon Lady muttering in your ear? Talking things out with a supportive person. Utilize your helpful coping skills. Reminding yourself that you are human and make mistakes just like everyone else. Working on your positive or neutral self-talk (the one thing I tell myself when I make a mistake is "I'm silly. I'm not stupid").

Caveats and Triggers

The biggest potential trigger: this movie is about death and has a (non-gory) scene where Daniel is killed by a bus. You may be triggered if someone you love has died in a violent or traumatic way, or if you were in a serious car crash. Another possible trigger: a short scene from when Daniel was a toddler when his dad is yelling at his mom, being emotionally abusive, and almost hits her.

My only caveats: some of the foreign-born characters seem to act more cartoonishly than their

American counterparts, and while all the people who die in the western U.S. end up in Judgment City, there are almost no minorities among them that we see.

Fun Facts

Actor/Writer/Director Albert Brooks' father, Harry Einstein, was a comedian, and his mother, Thelma Leeds, was an actress and singer. They named him Albert Einstein (which is just cruel). He changed his name in his teens. He claims that neither of his parents gave him a straight answer as to why exactly they named him Albert Einstein. I'm not sure why he chose Brooks, but it has a nice ring to it.

Brooks grew up with his best friend Rob Reiner, director of modern classics like *The Princess Bride*, (see Chapter 16) and *When Harry Met Sally ...* (see Chapter 19) and made it his personal mission to get Reiner's dad, comedy legend Carl Reiner, to laugh. Carl would say on talk shows that Brooks was the funniest person alive—starting when Brooks was in his teens.

Brooks used to call up his friends at home and tell them to turn on their TV. He would instruct them to turn it to a certain channel, and then they would watch a program together while discussing it. Interestingly, in a scene from *When Harry Met Sally...*, (see Chapter

19) Harry calls up Sally and they watch *Casablanca* together and discuss their thoughts about the movie.

Most of the characters Brooks has played have anxiety issues, including in all the movies he wrote, directed, and acted in at the same time. Why? I think there are at least two possible reasons. First of all, from what I can piece together, it appears that Albert Brooks has dealt with anxiety issues since he was 6. His dad got seriously ill around that time, and Brooks was worried that his dad would die—and he did when Brooks was 11. Secondly, he might have gotten typecast as a man who struggles with anxiety throughout most of his career because he plays these parts so well.

Brooks' most famous role of the last 30 years (and debatably his most famous role of all time) was as Marlin, Nemo's anxious dad in *Finding Nemo* and *Finding Dory*.

In a 2016 Rolling Stone interview, Brooks talked about the lasting impact of *Defending Your Life*: "I've gotten thousands and thousands of letters [from] people who had relatives that were dying, or they were dying themselves, and the movie made them feel better. I guess it's because it presents some possibility that doesn't involve clouds and ghostly images. So, this thing never goes away. It's a quarter of a century, but

I don't think the idea behind the subject is ever going to change."[40]

In the movie, Julia and Daniel visit the Past Lives Pavilion, where they can view who they were previously. While Julia sees her past self as a medieval knight that looks heroic, Daniel sees a man running for his life, from what we do not know. Their host at the Pavilion, and famous real-life believer in past lives, is Shirley MacLaine. This was one of Brooks' favorite scenes in the movie and mine as well.

---

[40] Wood 2016

CHAPTER 16

The Princess Bride
(1987)

CAST:

Cary Elwes—Westley

Mandy Patinkin—Inigo Montoya

André the Giant—Fezzik

Robin Wright—Buttercup/
The Princess Bride

Wallace Shawn—Vizzini

Chris Sarandon—Prince Humperdinck

Christopher Guest—Count Rugen

DIRECTED BY:

Rob Reiner

WRITING CREDITS:

Screenplay by: William Goldman

Based on the novel *The Princess Bride: S. Morgenstern's Classic Tale of True Love and High Adventure* by William Goldman

Plot Summary

A grandfather reads a rollicking adventure called *The Princess Bride* to his grandson when the lad is home sick from school. The story is of Buttercup and Westley, two young lovers who are torn apart when he is (or is he?) killed by pirates. Years later, Buttercup has reluctantly agreed to marry the evil Prince Humperdinck. She is then kidnapped by three men: Vizzini, who thinks he is the greatest genius the world has ever seen; Inigo, a Spaniard bent on revenging his father's death; and Fezzik, a gentle but incredibly strong giant with a true sense of honor.

A man in black pursues them as he is determined to rescue Buttercup from the trio. This man turns out to be Westley, who has not been killed after all. (There is so much more to this jam-packed story that I frankly wasn't sure how long a description I should give. In case you haven't had the delight of watching this movie, I'll let you discover the rest yourself.)

My Thoughts on This Movie

My favorite character is Fezzik. He is loyal to a fault, smarter than people give him credit for, and a total sweetheart. He always plays fair. He and Inigo make the perfect team no matter whether they are playing rhyming games, looking out for one another, or finding people hidden in trees. I aim to be as loyal, clever, and kind as Fezzik.

My second favorite is Inigo, a master fencer and a mostly serious individual, though he has some silliness in him. He will do anything and give up everything to get his revenge on the six-fingered man who killed his father, but, like Fezzik, is also devoted to his friends. His father, though dead, is a guiding force in his life. My father is very much alive, and he is also a guiding force in my life.

Outside of the main characters, there are some parts I consider "major minor characters" that I adore. Let me tell you what I mean by major minor. These are characters that appear in only one or two scenes but are still important in some way to the story.

My favorite major minor characters are Miracle Max (Billy Crystal) and The Impressive Clergyman (Peter Falk). I'm a devoted Crystal fan, and he does not disappoint as a man who thinks he has lost his talent for miracling. Almost all of Crystal's lines were improvised! He truly is a comedy genius. Peter Falk, with just eight lines, manages to sneak in 15 w's into words that don't have them, steal the scene, and inspire real-life couples to have someone quote his lines at weddings.

On my latest rewatch, I was the most disappointed in the character of Westley. He thinks he's smarter and better than everyone. In his anger at Buttercup's promise to marry the prince (even though she thought he was dead), he gets nasty. In his favor: he is a natural leader because of his charisma, his intellect, and his ability to find people's strengths.

I find it hard to believe that Buttercup doesn't recognize Westley—but then I usually do in movies when a mask that doesn't completely cover the face is involved. Would I recognize someone I loved if they had a mask on? (I wonder if you have ever been fooled by a person you know who is wearing half a mask. Well, perhaps at a masquerade? This is such a popular movie trope that people are fooled by masks, even if that person has the same voice and build. So many superhero movies would fall apart if partial masks didn't work in fictional worlds.)

How Watching This Movie Can Affect Our Mental Health

I discovered in college that watching this movie was helpful during my manic episodes. This was the first aha moment in discovering that a movie could help me in this way. When I was in the middle of a manic episode, my mind was going a thousand miles a minute. It was nearly impossible to concentrate on anything for very long. I couldn't read, I could barely have an intelligent conversation (or any at all, really), and even watching movies new to me was difficult as I couldn't follow the storyline very well.

What I *could* do was be soothed by watching movies like this one. I could not only be taken to the time and place of this fairy tale, but I could also be taken to the time and place of my childhood, feeling safe while watching a delightful movie. My mental health wasn't exactly great, even when I was a kid. Who wouldn't want to go to a comforting place, if only in their mind?

Do you have comfort movies? Ones that, when you watch them you feel like you're hugging a teddy bear? If you rewatch them, you likely will experience the same warm glow as you had before. They could be any sort of movie, from goofy comedies to dark dramas. I often ask people what their favorite movies are—but what I'm really trying to get at is their comfort movies, and I usually lead the conversation around to that.

What surprises me is the number of people who say that their favorites are thriller or horror movies. It just seems so strange to me that these often dark and violent movies could soothe anyone's soul. My theory on this is that either they watched a lot of horror or thriller films growing up, so it was ingrained in them to continue to love these types of movies, or that they revel in the visceral reactions they experience while watching them, or both. I won't judge you for your comfort movies, no matter how light or dark they are, or whether they were critically acclaimed, or if I found a significant ick factor in them.

Caveats and Triggers

I have only one caveat for this movie: that the only major female character is a dim-witted damsel in distress. There are so many times she must be rescued, often because she just doesn't know what she is doing, or she believes what Prince Humperdinck tells her when he is obviously lying. Yes, I know this is a fairy tale, where female leads are overwhelmingly damsels in distress—at least in the ones I have read or seen. I just can't help thinking how awesome the movie could have been with a warrior Buttercup. (At least I got to see Robin Wright in full warrior mode in *Wonder Woman*.) While the violence in *The Princess Bride* is cartoonish, it could conceivably be triggering. This includes the kidnapping I mentioned before, one torture scene, and many parts where characters are nearly killed, either by humans, animals, or nature itself.

Fun Facts

All of these facts came from Cary Elwes' book *As You Wish: Inconceivable Tales from the Making of The Princess Bride*.

For the sword fighting scene, Mandy Patinkin (Inigo) trained for six months and Cary Elwes (Westley) trained for four months before filming, and they practiced during any free moments while filming. The only parts of the fight where a stunt double was used were for the three acrobatic moves (two flips and a somersault) that happened during the scene. Otherwise, the actors were in every frame of the scene. Even the most famous swashbuckling actors like Errol Flynn always used stunt doubles during a sizeable portion of their scenes. It's even more impressive when you realize they had to learn to sword fight both right- and left-handed. All the fencing terms they refer to in the scene are real.

Some people on first meeting André the Giant would freak the heck out due to his size. Robin Wright was one of them—she ran away from him when she first met him, purely on instinct. On the second meeting, she warmed emotionally to this very sweet man. While filming the movie, the weather on location was sometimes very cold, and when Robin Wright was freezing, André would put his hand on her head to warm her up. His hand was so large it covered her entire head and it always did the trick.

During the shooting of the Miracle Max scene, the cast and crew had a horrible time stopping themselves from giggling during Billy Crystal's three straight days of improvising. The director had to leave the set and watch from a monitor as he was ruining takes with his mirth. They had to replace Elwes with a dummy in some takes as he was shaking with silent laughter. Patinkin managed to keep a straight face, but he was clenching his torso so hard to keep the laughter in that he bruised a rib.

While the movie has countless famous fans, the most surprising may be Pope John Paul II. Elwes found this out in 1988 when he and his mother had an audience with the then Pope.

Oh, and I found this out on my own: There was a CBS show that was on for one season in 2005 called *Pope John Paul II* and guess who played the pope as a young man? Cary Elwes.

CHAPTER 17

Big Business
(1988)

CAST:

Bette Midler—Sadie Shelton/Sadie Ratliff

Lily Tomlin—Rose Shelton/Rose Ratliff

Fred Ward—Roone Dimmick

Edward Herrmann—Graham Sherbourne

Daniel Gerroll—Chuck

DIRECTED BY:

Jim Abrahams

WRITING CREDITS:

Written by: Dori Pierson and Marc Rubel

Plot Summary

A very rich couple, Hunt and Binky Shelton, are from New York City. They get lost in rural West Virginia trying to find their friends' vacation home. Binky, 40 weeks pregnant, suddenly goes into labor. Frantically trying to find a hospital, they are told there is one 40 miles away, but they don't have time to get there. They find out about a hospital three miles away in a town called Jupiter Hollow, but there's a catch— it's only for people who work at Hollowmade, the local factory. The husband ends up buying the company so his wife can give birth in Jupiter Hollow, and she has identical twins.

At the same time, a local couple (the Ratliffs) are also having identical twins at the same hospital. Due to an inept nurse, the two sets of twins get mixed up—one Shelton baby (Sadie) goes with the Ratliffs, and one Ratliff baby (Rose) goes with the Sheltons. To confuse things further, both sets of girls are named Sadie and Rose.

Flash forward and Rose Shelton (who I will call city Rose), living in New York, feels out of place and pines for rural life (where she should rightly be living). Sadie Ratliff (country Sadie) in Jupiter Hollow wants to live in New York—which is where she should have been. Sadie Shelton (city Sadie), very comfortable and just where she should be, is all about the money and plans on selling Hollowmade so the land can be strip-mined. Rose Ratliff (country Rose), also comfortable where she is, decides to go to New York to stop her town from being destroyed—and her Sadie comes along as she has plans to move to the big city. Hilarity ensues and mistaken identities abound.

My Thoughts on This Movie

I would wager that *Big Business* has the least name recognition of any of the movies in this book. That's why I am beyond delighted when someone I meet has seen it. Even if you, dear reader, have seen it, I bet you haven't seen it since the '80s or '90s.

At first glance, you might think that both the Roses are the better set of twins, and there is something seriously wrong with the Sadies. City Sadie is the real baddie, who would throw anyone and everyone under the bus to get more money. She is just cruel to pretty much everyone. Country Sadie hates everything about her hometown and can be selfish. City Rose loves people and animals, and country Rose wants to fight tooth and nail for her hometown.

After two recent rewatches, I saw that two of the reasons behind city Sadie's behavior were this: she was raised by a stuck-up, mean, and materialistic mother she idolized, and she is constantly going on extreme diets because she is self-conscious about her weight. She insults herself because she thinks she weighs too much. She is also jealous of her sister, who eats all the time but remains thin.

Going back to the country sisters: while country Sadie can be selfish, she can also be genuinely sweet—sometimes sweeter than her sister Rose. Country Rose is mostly an assertive person with a deep love for her hometown, but she can get aggressive and judgy at times. Even city Rose is not perfect—she never wants to stick up for herself and is easily distracted.

Bette Midler and Lily Tomlin were two of my favorite actresses as a child. They were—and are—so talented and funny. I have always loved Midler's voice, and near the beginning she does a fun song and dance number in the movie, which opens with her milking a cow, and then doing some fancy footwork. The number happens during a fundraiser in support of her small town. She then does a different version of the song later when she's exploring New York and dancing to steel drums.

Nobody (including the two sets of twins) knows there are really two Sadies and two Roses at the hotel. All four characters' love interests confuse one of the twins for the other. Co-workers, hotel staff, and others wonder what the heck is going on.

There's also a lovely gay couple, Graham and Chuck, who work for the Sheltons. I'm thankful that these characters are just shown as people, not caricatures, and I can see no homophobic messages in the movie. This makes sense as Tomlin is gay, and Midler has always had a huge gay following. I didn't catch that the two men were lovers when I first saw it as a young child, but I caught on during a rewatch a few years later.

Why do I love this movie so much? It's about four women who kick butt. They all have different talents, and in general are three-dimensional characters. None of them is a flawless beauty. I see a lot of myself in city Rose. We both love animals, really enjoy desserts, can be very passive at times, and often have our heads in the clouds.

The movie is about not always feeling comfortable where you are. It's about the power of sisters. It's about distinct types of love. It's about the underdog, and that money can't buy everything. It shows the exhilaration of the city and the calm of the country.

The movie explores one of my favorite topics: nature vs. nurture. If both Sadies had grown up together in New York, would they have both been mean? If the Roses had both grown up in West Virginia, would they both have been assertive?

On one hand, usually identical twins separated at birth are much more alike than the twins in this movie, but those who grow up together tend to be even closer in personality. On the other hand, identical twins are not clones and can still have drastically different personalities whether they grew up together or not.

How Watching This Movie Can Affect Our Mental Health

As in *A League of Their Own*, this movie focuses on the relationship between sisters. This is a recurring theme in several of the movies in this section. Why do I keep going back to sisters? Because my sister is just that important to me.

Do you have a sibling whose personality is the opposite of yours? Have you ever felt confused about how you could possibly be related to this person? Not necessarily in a bad way, but in a way where you often have a challenging time figuring out where they're coming from and why they do the things they do? Both the Sadies and the Roses seem to feel this way about their sisters and can lead to long-standing conflicts between each pair. Perhaps you or your sibling have completely given up on trying to understand each other, or you even avoid each other as much as possible.

I read once that the longest familial relationship you typically will ever have in your life is the one you share with your sibling(s). It seems obvious, really, as they will be the only contemporaries you will have throughout your life. So, it is important and rewarding to have a positive kinship with your sibling(s). I encourage you to try and keep them in your life unless you have a toxic or abusive relationship.

My step-grandmother Bertha died in the spring of 2018 at the age of 96. She was incredibly close to her sister, Erma, since they both were young, even with a 13-year age difference. Bertha was widowed twice over, once at age 71 when her first husband died, and then at 81 when her second husband, my grandfather, died. Bertha had children (and eventually grandchildren and great-grandchildren) but there was one person who was 100% there for her almost her entire life: her best friend and sister, Erma. How amazing is that? (I've thought about Erma off and on, and how she is coping without Bertha.)

Remember how I said that city Sadie's meanness might be connected to her extreme dieting? I've been there. Then when I'm off the diet my irritability either vanishes or decreases significantly but I regain the weight. I've also been there about having a poor body image and a thin sister. It's hard not to compare yourself to your siblings. Do you have siblings who have qualities you wish you had? Perhaps you are jealous of them, or feel that you will never be as good as they are at something? It can take a toll on the relationship for sure.

Caveats and Triggers

Nada.

Fun Facts

Bette Midler, aka The Divine Miss M, has worked as an actress and a performer in movies, TV, and theater consistently (with a few short breaks here and there) since the early '60s. She is known for her unique voice and has performed at least one song in 12 of the feature films she has acted in. According to the Internet Movie Database (*IMDB.com*) she has 96 soundtrack credits and 43 acting credits in TV and movies. She's won three competitive Grammys, three Emmys, one Tony and three Golden Globe awards. Lily Tomlin is no slouch either, appearing in movies, TV, plays, and releasing comedy albums since the '60s. She has six competitive Emmys, a Tony, and a Grammy.

In a 1988 *Good Morning America* interview with the two leads, Bette Midler gushed about Lily Tomlin and called her a pioneer. Tomlin's character, city Rose, eats constantly, and Midler said during the interview that her only suggestion for Tomlin was that she shouldn't really have eaten the food her character was eating as it would make her sick. Tomlin told her that she wasn't usually eating the food but spitting it out (like the vast majority of actors do). She said that she only would swallow the food if it was "well-made" and "high-quality."[41]

Big Business is basically a distant cousin of one of my favorite Shakespearean plays, *The Comedy of Errors.* Here's a description of the play from Washington, D.C.'s The Shakespeare Theatre Company: "Two sets of twins, each with the same name—what could go wrong? Everything, apparently. Leave logic behind and delight in the confusion…where servants misplace their masters, wives overlook their husbands, and sons forget their fathers. The blunders double, triple and cube until chaos reigns…" [42]

[41] YouTube 2013
[42] Shakespeare Theatre Company 2018

CHAPTER 18

Tommy Boy
(1995)

CAST:

Chris Farley—Tommy

David Spade—Richard

Brian Dennehy—Big Tom

Rob Lowe—Paul Barish (uncredited)

Bo Derek—Beverly

Julie Warner—Michelle

Dan Aykroyd—Zalinsky

DIRECTED BY:

Peter Segal

WRITING CREDITS:

Written by: Bonnie Turner & Terry Turner

Plot Summary

Tommy is a lovable, friendly, and chubby guy. He graduates (after seven years) from Marquette University in Milwaukee, Wisconsin, and goes back home to Sandusky, Ohio, to work at his dad's company, Callahan Auto Parts. There he finds out that his dad is about to be remarried and that he will gain a new stepmother and stepbrother. At the wedding reception, his dad—who was also his best friend—dies of a heart attack. Tommy is forced to go on a sales trip with his dad's smart and snarky chief assistant, Richard, to save the company.

My Thoughts on This Movie

I've been a fan of Chris Farley since he started on Saturday Night Live. He oozed talent. He was also reportedly a very sweet man. He was never so embarrassed about his weight to stop his gift of physical humor. However, he did have some body issues. He was overweight his entire life and was bullied for much of it.

I wonder how he felt, as a person, to constantly get fat jokes lobbed at him during this movie. Did it contribute to his mental health issues? He dealt with depression and substance abuse issues for much of his adult life, though he was reportedly sober during the filming of this movie.

David Spade's Richard is spiteful and mean—but he's like that because he's jealous of Tommy and because he uses sarcasm and insults to protect himself from getting hurt. I think it can be good to have rude and insensitive characters like Richard in movies. By learning why the characters are the way they are, you might get some insight into the backstories of why mean people you know are the way they are. This might help in learning exactly how to deal with real-life jerks. Everyone, real or imagined, has a backstory.

Really, Richard and Tommy complete each other—Richard is all about the book learning but has no social skills, and Tommy is great with people but lacking in intellect. They need each other, and neither can complete their mission without the other. I've always wondered—what if I was more like Tommy than Richard? What if I gained social skills, but wasn't book smart anymore? Would I be happier? Tommy is much happier with his life than Richard is, even though Tommy can sometimes get down on himself.

You get a fun bad guy in Rob Lowe, who was a great '90s bad guy in this and other movies like *Wayne's World*. He plays an egocentric character nicely, and his face can look menacing if he wants it to. He can embrace his dark side. He can do physical humor as well, which keeps things from getting too dark. Nothing like slapstick to keep scariness to a reasonable level.

How Watching This Movie Can Affect Our Mental Health

I identify with Tommy because I've been bullied both as a child and as an adult for my weight. I've been judged throughout my life for it, even by those closest to me. I have a complex about it like Tommy does. I've played the buffoon on and off throughout my life, and I'm pretty good at making people laugh at my buffoonery.

Did you get bullied because of your weight, or something else? Are you still carrying around the feeling that you aren't good enough because of the way people used to treat you—or still treat you?

I encourage you to realize what your gifts are and play to them. I'm never going to be a supermodel, but I go out of my way to be a kind person. I love to enliven conversations through humor, and I always try to see the good in any situation. I push for the end to the stigma against those with mental health issues. What gifts do you have?

It's also important to be introspective so you can consciously know where any baggage you might have comes from. I think it can make things a bit better. I know that there was one toxic "friendship" I had in middle school that led to the worst of the body image issues. This person had an eating disorder, and to make herself feel better she would tell me to weigh myself and then she would weigh herself—she always weighed less, and she would make fun of me for that. She would also take a string and put it around my arms or legs, and then measure that against hers, and make fun of me. This went on for at least a year.

She had some serious issues. Was she a terrible person? No, but she was broken. Hurt people hurt people. So, I'm not bad because of my weight. You're not bad because of any of your perceived imperfections. I promise.

Caveats and Triggers

I have more caveats with this movie than any other one in this section, so I had to really weigh the positives versus the negatives. It boils down to this: the fat jokes, and to a lesser extent, the "Tommy is stupid" jokes invoke a delicate situation. I would imagine some mean people watching this and saying, "Well, it's okay to laugh at people because they're fat or dumb because they're already making fun of themselves!" Other people might say, "Well I guess people should laugh at me because of how I look or act." So, it's tricky, you see. I included this for the people who can relate to Tommy and see that there is so much more to him than how he appears.

Fun Facts

Farley did all his own stunts, including being hit in the face with a two-by-four by Spade—though something went wrong with this stunt. Director Peter Segal revealed that at one point Spade accidentally hit Farley with the business end of the two-by-four, not the padded part. I was unable to find out whether any mark was left.

Roger Ebert disliked the movie so much he put it on his "Most Hated List" under "Alleged Comedies." He had this to say in his 1995 review: "No one is funny in 'Tommy Boy.' There are no memorable lines. None of the characters is interesting except for the enigmatic figure played by Rob Lowe, who seems to have wandered over from 'Hamlet.'"[43]

Obviously, I disagree with him, just like I disagree with his decision to put the awful *Lost in Translation* on his list of the 300+ greatest movies of all time.

---

[43] Ebert 1995

There are a lot of similarities between Tommy and Farley. They both went to Marquette University and played rugby. Farley, like Tommy, would make fun of himself for his weight and because he thought he was stupid. Farley went to work for his dad at their family business, Scotch Oil Company, which was in his hometown of Madison, Wisconsin, just like Tommy went to work for his dad after college. Scotch Oil, like Callahan Auto Parts, was family owned for decades.

Another reason I'm a devoted Farley fan: I also grew up in Madison, and my house was less than a mile from the Catholic high school Farley attended.

CHAPTER 19

When Harry Met Sally… (1989)

CAST:

Billy Crystal—Harry Burns

Meg Ryan—Sally Albright

Carrie Fisher—Marie

Bruno Kirby—Jess

DIRECTED BY:

Rob Reiner

WRITING CREDITS:

Written by: Nora Ephron

Plot Summary

Harry and Sally, recent University of Chicago graduates, meet when Harry's girlfriend, who is friends with Sally, suggests that they drive together to New York City from Chicago, where they both (separately) want to make a new life. Sally thinks that Harry is ill-mannered, strange, and a bit of a creep. Harry thinks that Sally is too uptight and naïve. They part and then meet again years later when they are both traveling and on the same flight, but again, things don't seem to have changed much in the way they view each other. Years after that, both single, they meet up again and become close friends and confidants.

My Thoughts on This Movie

I think this is the most true-to-life and believable rom-com I've ever seen. So much of that is because it's based on the real-life experiences of screenwriter Nora Ephron, director Rob Reiner, and producer Andrew Scheinman. It has been spelled out by both the writer and the director, when it came to their personalities, Ephron is Sally and Reiner is Harry. Billy Crystal felt that Harry was so much like Reiner that Crystal had to push to add his own ideas about how to portray the character.

Ephron, known throughout her decades-long career as a journalist, essayist, author, screenwriter, and director for her humor and feminism, was able to create a subtly feminist character with Sally. This character is in all ways equal to Harry. Her thoughts, actions, and emotions are just as complex as Harry's. Sally is neither an angel nor a devil, but simply a woman.

I know that there are people who believe that feminism is a dirty word. That all feminists are man haters, and harshly judge other women in many different ways. Well, that's not what Ephron's feminism is about. None of the women in the movie hate men. They may get frustrated with individual men, but they don't hate them because they are male. The female characters aren't trying to tell each other how they should or shouldn't behave as women.

The most iconic scene in the movie takes place in a deli. Sally talks about how she is disgusted with the way Harry often treats women he goes out with, and how he talks about them. He had told her about how he doesn't like to sleep over at a woman's house, or at least he always tries to leave very early in the morning, making a lame or fake excuse for leaving. He pins the fault that he does this not on himself, but on his belief that most women are too needy, and he doesn't want to have to deal with what he thinks are insecure women.

When Harry implies that he shows women such a good time that it's okay to lie about having to leave after sex, Sally blows that idea out of the water. While having lunch in a deli, Sally fakes an orgasm to prove to Harry that it is something that is easy to do and that women can do it whenever they feel like it. She wants to show him that he can never know for sure that he has shown them a good time because they could just be faking.

I believe in the same brand of feminism as Ephron—that we are all human beings and that our gender says nothing about who we are at our core. Let all the stereotypes fall away and things will seem so much clearer and better. You will find this same brand of feminism in *Little Women* (see Chapter 21). I think that my feminist thinking was further solidified through watching movies like these. In fact, most of the movies I chose have at least a hint of this belief I have about gender.

Because so much of the film is based on true stories and emotions, the characters are all three dimensional and painfully human. Like all my favorite rom-coms, this one shows me that romance is not dead. I don't mean the buying flowers kind of romance, but the deeply passionate kind. I think it can be hard to show truly deep passion with fake or one-dimensional characters.

You may have noticed that both Meg Ryan and Billy Crystal are in other movies in this book: Ryan in *Joe Versus the Volcano* (see Chapter 20) and Crystal in *The Princess Bride* (see Chapter 16). Director Rob Reiner also helmed *The Princess Bride*. There are certain actors, directors, and screenwriters that often appear in more than one of my favorite movies. It makes sense, as they have a certain style, are attracted to projects that have a least a little something in common, or, like Reiner and Crystal, they overlap because they enjoy working together. When I think of *When Harry Met Sally…*, *Joe Versus the Volcano*, and *The Princess Bride*, and many others in this book, one word I could use to describe them is clever.

If you want more Meg Ryan/Nora Ephron pairings, I suggest their movies *Sleepless in Seattle* and *You've Got Mail*. In addition, the divine Meryl Streep—who co-stars in *Defending Your Life* (Chapter 15)—and Ephron have collaborated on *Silkwood*, *Heartburn*, and *Julie & Julia*. (Streep's portrayal of Julia Child is one of my favorites of her film roles of the last 25 years. If you haven't seen this gem, do so. She is hilarious, charismatic, and simply perfect.)

Crystal is adept at all kinds of comedy. His character Miracle Max in *The Princess Bride* is like a stand-up comedian—the formula is just joke after joke after joke. Harry is obviously a much more complex character, and Crystal plays him perfectly. The actor had established his comedic chops years before this 1989 film, and I love his humor dearly. Meg Ryan, however, was in her first lead role and hadn't been known for her comedic gifts before performing in the movie. She had mostly supporting parts before this film. You might think that she is the "straight woman" in this movie.

She is so much more, however, as you see in the deli scene and throughout the movie. Rewatching the movie I also found her other depths. I encourage you to watch Sally's eyes closely in every scene. Sally will say or do something that seems true, but her eyes can betray her real feelings. This (and everything else I mentioned) is the reason I think it was her best acting role in any movie I've ever seen her in.

(Yes, this includes all the dramas. I get really bent out of shape when people assume that the best acting comes out of dramas and not comedies. Many actors and writers who have worked on both comedic and dramatic films say that comedy is more difficult to pull off, including Oscar winner Michael Caine who said, "Comedy is harder to do than drama. You can make anyone burst into tears but trying to get a laugh is murder.").[44]

[44] Cline 2017

Another interesting thing about this movie is that we see Harry and Sally from the ages of 22 to 34. You see the characters grow into adulthood. Their ideas and ideals grow out of that change. The rigid thinking of youth turns into a more accepting and broad-minded thinking as they grow older. All the main characters in the movie can sometimes be jaded about dating, but they are also able to develop deeper bonds in both their romantic and platonic relationships.

Finally, you get the bonus of the amazing Carrie Fisher in this movie, who plays Sally's best friend, Marie. You see her character's desperate hope in the beginning that her love interest will leave his wife for her, and then punishing herself that she has this hope. She meets Harry's (single) best friend Jess, and when they get together, their relationship is just as nuanced as Harry and Sally's. You root for Marie since you know how unhappy and angry she was at the beginning of the movie.

How Watching This Movie Can Affect Our Mental Health

I feel my anxiety and depression melting away within a minute of starting to watch this film. I really recommend that you think about what your favorite movies were as a child or a teen and watch them again now. You might find the same decrease in symptoms that I experienced. Another perk might be that you can feel your soul just start to glow with warm memories of your past viewings.

I will warn you that rewatching some movies you loved as a kid can end badly. You might find that there are themes, scenes or characters that just make you feel icky—like racist stereotypes or gay slurs. Or you might realize that the movie is so awful your perception of it changes. So, you might want to proceed with caution depending on the movie. If you're feeling unsure about whether you will still love it, you can search for clips, trailers, reviews, or articles online before you smash your lovely memories to bits if it turns out to be terrible.

A big reason why I included *When Harry Met Sally...* in this book is because, out of every movie we watched together, this is the one that my sister and I came back to time and time again. It is the one that we agreed we loved equally. Jane was quoting it and talking about it when I first told her about the book, even before I decided it would be included. Watching it together in the past was a wonderful way to bond with her.

Are there particular movies that you have watched countless times with family members or friends? I encourage you to watch these movies again with them to reinforce or restart a positive relationship. If you can't do that, just quoting the movie back and forth can be a magical experience. If they have passed on, you can watch the movie in remembrance of that cherished person.

I think the power of friendship is the main theme. A friend can be the most important person in your life. There's a lot of talk in the movie about Harry and Sally being "just friends." However, I really dislike that term. Friends can be the most important people in your life regardless of whether you are in a romantic relationship. It's very common for people to have friends who have been in their lives longer than their romantic partners. It's healthy to have strong friendships outside of a monogamous romantic partnership so you don't solely rely on one person for all your emotional needs.

I wouldn't be where I am today without my friends, and I thank them for what they have done for me. Sometimes single people feel that they "need" a partner to be whole, someone who will support them all the time. What all of us really need is human connection. It doesn't have to be romantic in nature, but it does need to be healthy.

A final note: I can very much relate to Harry's occasional depressive moods and beliefs. He thinks about death a lot, can be very cynical, worries if he will ever find the "right" person for him, and carries a lot of dread with him. One of the things that exacerbated Harry's issues was that not only did his ex-wife divorce him and say some very hurtful things when she told him the marriage was over, but he found out that she was cheating on him as well.

From the research I've done on the film, I found that director Rob Reiner went through similar dark moods and beliefs before the production of the film— though I found no evidence that his first wife was ever that cruel to him. (He met his current wife, Michele Singer, during the production, so he's presumably no longer worrying about meeting the "right" person. From what I could glean from various interviews, it seems that his mental health has improved over the years, but there's no way to know for sure.)

My depression, like most people's, comes with an unhealthy dose of dread that I also carry around. The what-ifs, the if-onlys, the feeling that things will never work out for me. Do you ever feel that way? I would never tell you or myself that this isn't a logical way to feel, that you should just buck up and smile and everything will be better.

However, when I feel this way, I go to my coping skills (like watching movies) and it often helps me. When you are in the depths of despair, try something simple that you enjoy doing. It might help.

Caveats and Triggers

Nada.

Fun Facts

Nora Ephron, like Sally, is a foodie and orders exactly like Sally does, with everything to an exact specification. Rob Reiner loved this so much about Ephron that he made it part of the movie.

There are endless hilarious quotes in this movie, but the one it's known for is during the deli scene, and is spoken by the director's mother, Estelle Reiner. The quote is #33 on the American Film Institute's list of the 100 best movie quotes of all time.[45]

Princess Diana was at the London premiere of the movie and wanted to laugh out loud many times while watching the film, but she told Billy Crystal after the movie was over that she had to hold herself back, being royalty and all. She decided to have her own private screening at Buckingham Palace with her friends, and presumably was able to laugh at scenes like the one that takes place at the deli.

Carrie Fisher loved being in the movie and felt that the character of Marie was so like her that she barely had to act.

---

[45] Firstenberg 2005

CHAPTER 20

Joe Versus the Volcano
(1990)

CAST:

Tom Hanks—Joe

Meg Ryan—DeDe/Angelica/Patricia

Lloyd Bridges—Graynamore

Robert Stack—Dr. Ellison

DIRECTED BY:

John Patrick Shanley

WRITING CREDITS:

Written by: John Patrick Shanley

Plot Summary

Joe Banks hates his job, the decrepit factory he works in, and dealing with his jerk-face boss. He has felt sick for many years and spends all his money on doctors although he has never been diagnosed with anything. He goes to see a new doctor (Dr. Ellison) who tells him he has a "brain cloud" that was found through all the testing. According to the doctor, Joe will die from the "brain cloud" in six months, but he will not actually have any noticeable symptoms before he passes.

A rich man named Graynamore hires him to go to a small island and jump, willingly, into a volcano. In exchange, Joe will receive the best life has to offer for his last months on earth and be a hero to the people who live on this small island by appeasing their volcano god through his ultimate sacrifice. Over the course of the movie, Joe spends time with three very different women—his co-worker DeDe, and Angelica and Patricia (two half-sisters), who all look almost exactly the same.

My Thoughts on This Movie

Many people don't know it, but this, and not *Sleepless in Seattle*, was the original pairing of Meg Ryan and Tom Hanks. If you liked it and/or the other movie they co-starred in, *You've Got Mail,* yay! You can watch another pairing of these two intensely likable actors. It is far and away my favorite of the three movies. It was one of the first DVDs I ever bought.

This may be one of the weirdest romantic comedies I have ever seen, and that's why I love it. If I wanted to put this movie in a box, I would call it magical realism, which is a genre that is set in the real world but has magical or fantastic elements.

On rewatching, it was even weirder and darker than I remembered, and I'm a bit curious as to why it was such a favorite of both mine and my sister's when we were young. It's been at least 10 years since I last saw it. I think a big part of the reason was the Hanks/Ryan pairing, and I have always liked movies that have some fantastical element.

One of the things I had forgotten—and one of the reasons I'm sure my child-self loved this movie—is Hanks' impeccable physical comedy. The laughs really come more from this than anything else. You can see this type of comedy from Hanks in *A League of Their Own* (see Chapter 14) and in two other movies I adore—*Big* and *Forrest Gump.*

I have an intense fear of sharks. It stems from when I was 5 and my family was at Universal Studios. During their most famous ride, the shark from *Jaws* pops out of the water. I really thought that shark was going to eat me—it scared me to death. I'm still afraid of sharks.

Sometimes, when I'm in the deep end of a pool, I look below me to check if there's a mechanical shark in the water. There is a very slight possibility that a mechanical shark would be in a pool, as you can buy them to scare people while swimming. I've had countless nightmares about mechanical sharks since that horrible ride.

Anyway, there's a scene where I know that Joe is going to catch a shark. I literally covered my eyes and then peeked through as I decided it was more important to watch Hanks' brilliant antics while trying to reel in what he thought would be some awesome giant fish than freak out over the shark. I still saw the shark because—fun fact—peeking out through your fingers does not mean that you can't see the movie. The good thing about the scene is that it looked more like a monster than a shark, and I'm usually not scared of monsters.

Not every actor of any gender can excel at playing more than one character in a movie, let alone three like Meg Ryan does here! As we saw with *Big Business* (Chapter 17), it's a lot of work to play multiple characters, and it shows true talent. Ryan starts off as Joe's coworker, mousy and quiet DeDe. Then it's on to half-sisters Angelica and Patricia, who share the same father, Graynamore, who is bankrolling the trip to the island. Angelica is a ditzy and fragile artist. Patricia, the character who has the most screen time of the three, is conflicted, headstrong, and confused over her feelings for Joe.

I was so sad when the movie was over. It went by in a flash!

How Watching This Movie Can Affect Our Mental Health

Joe has physical symptoms such as frequent sore throats and headaches that cause him to go to doctors. Dr. Ellison, who diagnoses him with the "brain cloud," labels him a hypochondriac as no doctor could find anything physically wrong with him except the brain cloud. Ellison suggests that Joe developed hypochondria due to the trauma he experienced nearly dying several times when he was a firefighter.

I found it interesting that Ellison didn't shame Joe or not believe him as there has always been so much stigma around what used to be called hypochondria, or illness anxiety disorder as it is known now. That Ellison didn't say Joe should just "snap out of it" is refreshing.

Whether it was hypochondria or PTSD (my money is on PTSD due to his traumas and symptoms), what matters is that Ellison didn't tell Joe it was all in his head.

When I had my first anxiety attack at 16, I thought I was dying. An ambulance was called because I felt like I couldn't breathe. I was taken to the ER, and they found nothing wrong physically. They treated me like I was faking. How I wish they had gotten a mental health worker in to see what was going on. It's obvious to me looking back that I was having an anxiety attack, and it should have been obvious to them. When I first got diagnosed with depression, I was lifted up by the fact that the therapist actually believed there was something going on and that I needed help.

Have you told a medical professional or counselor about your mental health issues and been dismissed? If so, that sucks, and I wish that it hadn't happened. I encourage you to talk to another doctor or therapist and let them know what is going on. It can be scary when you have already been written off to put yourself out there again. Just know there are so many people who work in mental health who want to help you and see you succeed.

I see the main theme of this movie as "what would you do if you had nothing to lose?" Joe has been diagnosed with an incurable condition. He realizes he doesn't need his crappy job. He finds out that he might be able to live in high style until his death and even be seen as a hero once again, like he was in his firefighting days.

I decided to write this book when I realized that I had nothing to lose if I did so. I have been immensely happy throughout this process. I'm in no way discounting anyone's struggles of any kind, but I encourage you to think about what you would do if you had nothing left to lose.

Caveats and Triggers

There are no triggers, but spoiler alert! Joe and Patricia eventually get to the island. Two white actors, Abe Vigoda and Nathan Lane, play two of the island's inhabitants (and the ones with the most lines.) They aren't in brown face, but it would have been nice to have some Pacific Islanders in these parts.

Fun Facts

According to Roger Ebert: "What's strongest about the movie is that it does possess a philosophy, an idea about life. The idea is... that at night, in those corners of our minds we deny by day, magical things can happen in the moon shadows. And if they can't,

a) they should, and b) we should always in any event act as if they can."[46]

Joe's company, American Panascope (which sells rectal probes), has a logo that looks like a zig-zagging line. The image shows up many times, such as in Joe's dreary path to the company, a wall in Joe's apartment, and a lightning bolt.

In one of the special features on the DVD I have, Hanks calls the movie an "existential comedy." Do you wonder what he might mean by that? I think Leah Schnelbach, staff writer at *Tor.com*, can explain—it's "actually an examination of morality, death, and more particularly the preparation for death that most people in the West do their best to avoid. The film celebrates and then subverts movie clichés to create a pointed commentary on what people value, and what they choose to ignore. Plus, it's also really funny!"[47]

---

[46] Ebert 1990
[47] Schnelbach 2017

CHAPTER 21

Little Women
(1994)

CAST:

Winona Ryder—Jo March

Trini Alvarado—Meg March

Claire Danes—Beth March

Kirsten Dunst—Younger Amy March

Samantha Mathis—Older Amy March

Susan Sarandon—Mrs. March

Christian Bale—Laurie

DIRECTED BY:

Gillian Armstrong

WRITING CREDITS:

Screenplay by: Robin Swicord

Based on the novel *Little Women* by:
Louisa May Alcott

Plot Summary

This is an adaptation of Louisa May Alcott's autobiographical novel *Little Women*. It focuses on four sisters and their beloved mother who are surviving and thriving in the small town of Concord, Massachusetts, throughout the Civil War and the years immediately afterward. The family must pull together emotionally and financially while their father is fighting as a Union soldier in the war.

There are some fights and frustrations, but the sisters are very close throughout all their time together. Everyone in the March family is a feminist due to their belief in transcendentalism, which means there is an emphasis on education for all genders and on the positive qualities of all people, with a de-emphasis on the importance of a pretty face. The men of their clan accept and celebrate the March women, while never trying to put them on a pedestal or undermine their gifts.

My Thoughts on This Movie

Transcendentalism is, according to the Oxford English Dictionary (OED):

1. An idealistic philosophical and social movement which developed in New England around 1836 in reaction to rationalism. Influenced by

romanticism, Platonism, and Kantian philosophy, it taught that divinity pervades all nature and humanity, and its members held progressive views on feminism and communal living. Ralph Waldo Emerson and Henry David Thoreau were central figures.

2. A system developed by Immanuel Kant, based on the idea that, in order to understand the nature of reality, one must first examine and analyze the reasoning process which governs the nature of experience.[48]

If the OED description of transcendentalism is a bit dense for your liking, here's a simpler explanation:

"Transcendentalism is a very formal word that describes a very simple idea. People, men and women equally, have knowledge about themselves and the world around them that 'transcends' or goes beyond what they can see, hear, taste, touch or feel."[49]

Ralph Waldo Emerson "believed that people were naturally good and that everyone's potential was limitless. He inspired his colleagues to look into themselves, into nature, into art, and through work for answers to life's most perplexing questions. His intellectual contributions to the philosophy of

---

[48] Oxford English Dictionary 2018
[49] USHistory.org 2018

transcendentalism inspired a uniquely American idealism and spirit of reform."[50]

The church I grew up in, Unity, has deep roots in transcendentalism. Co-founders of the church, Charles and Myrtle Fillmore, based Unity's tenets more on Emerson's work than any other. The church has been dismissed as a cult throughout its history by some because of beliefs it shares with transcendentalism, such as the "limitless potential" Emerson wrote about, looking within oneself for answers, and that God is kind and never wrathful.[51]

Little Women was one of the first movies I saw that really emphasized the kind of feminism I believe in. By that I mean the theory that all genders are equal and that it is of the utmost importance to treat people, no matter their gender, with respect. For instance, in the movie when a group of men is debating whether women should have the vote, Jo interjects that women should be able to vote not because they are more moral than men, but because they are people too. I do not believe, (and neither do the March women), that hating men is part of being a feminist.

I didn't fully grasp how dominant the theme of feminism was in the movie until my late teens or early

[50] USHistory.org 2018
[51] Hicks 2018

twenties. I have always believed, even as a child, that girls and women were in all ways equal to males. That was how I was raised, that's what I learned in school, and that's what the other adults in my world stressed to me.

It's another thing, however, to watch a movie like this that really can drive this point home, both consciously and unconsciously. If you believe in equality, this is the perfect movie to both watch yourself and to show your kids.

Another thing I like about this movie is the prominence of the theme that the best men are kind, caring, and never look down on women. The three most important suitors for three of the sisters are sweet men who are happy and willing to see the women they love as their equals.

Each sister is tested in some way. Meg must decide if having male attention, nice things and being beautiful are what she values the most. Jo is tested by her temper and other's reactions to her writing. Beth must battle illness. Amy is tested with her desire to marry a rich man even if she doesn't love him.

How Watching This Movie Can Affect Our Mental Health

Here is another movie that focuses on sisters. Unlike the other movies about sisters that show more conflict than harmony, much more of the story in this movie is about how these sisters band together, enjoy themselves, and protect each other. I aspire to have a relationship with my sister that is more like the March sisters in this respect.

In my most recent rewatch I felt my anxiety go down about 30 seconds into the opening credits of the movie. I've loved this film since I was in my early teens. It's like the warmest, softest blanket you could imagine. I love to cuddle up emotionally with this movie, and I think that you might too. It makes me feel safe.

As I mentioned in the *Inside Out* chapter, I never used to cry at movies. When I rewatched this movie in my late teens, it was the first time I remember crying during a film. If you have seen the movie, you can probably guess the scene. If not, it's just too big a spoiler to give away without a good reason. If what you are looking for is emotional release, you may find it in the scenes that are joyous, poignant, or a mix of both.

The hardest part of transcendentalism, at least for Jo, is the work of constantly focusing on perfecting your character. I find this difficult as well. I am a firm believer in continuously working on your character throughout your life, but I can easily get into shame spirals around this sort of thing. The problem with wanting to perfect your character is obvious: no one can be perfect. I especially relate to Jo in this challenge.

I also identify with Jo as we are both writers. The criticism of her writing, both from those close to her and from strangers, often causes her pain. It can be hard for me to accept any kind of criticism.

How do you respond to criticism? If it fills you with despair, you are in no way alone. It's okay to be sensitive about it, but I suggest not beating yourself up about it, and not metaphorically or literally beating the critic up over it. It's okay to take your sensitivity into account when it comes to how you act when you face criticism. Make sure you are taking care of yourself too.

Here's an example: I was working at a call center, and we were required to take documentation during calls. Everyone would get periodic reviews on our documentation. When I was told ahead of time what call was going to be reviewed, I knew that I was screwed. I had not done a good job. When I saw that the reviewer agreed with me, my first inclination was to think that I would be fired because of my mistakes.

The second was that the reviewer must really hate me because they listed more mistakes than I thought I had made.

I had to do a reality check: I had not done anything that would lose me the job, and the reviewer was just doing their job. I had made a mistake, and that was okay to do as long as I didn't make a habit of it.

I eventually let my anger towards myself go just to take care of myself, stay out of the shame spiral, and let go of all the anger I had toward the reviewer.

Caveats and Triggers

I personally have no caveats when it comes to recommending this movie. It is just about perfect in my eyes. Possible triggers could include: if you currently have family members or friends fighting in a war or conflict, and you know there is a chance they could die or be wounded. There is also a shot that lasts less than a minute of wounded men coming back from fighting in the Civil War. It's not gruesome but it could be a possible trigger.

Fun Facts

From my research, as of December 2018, I found 17 film or televised versions of *Little Women*, with one in the works. I'm so looking forward to the 2019 version, which will come out on Christmas Day, as it will star Saorise Ronan *(Lady Bird)* as Jo, Emma Watson as Meg, Laura Dern as Marmee, and Meryl Streep as Aunt March! *Lady Bird* director Greta Gerwig will be at the helm.

The 1994 version is crammed with stars of the '90s (with most of them still acting today): Susan Sarandon, Winona Ryder, Claire Danes, Kirsten Dunst, Christian Bale, Eric Stoltz, Gabriel Byrne, Trini Alvarado, and Samantha Mathis. John Neville (Mr. Laurence) had several smaller roles during that decade but is probably most famous for a movie that's dear to my heart, *The Adventures of Baron Munchausen*. As for Mary Wickes (Aunt March), she was in show business for nearly 60 years, and this was her last live-action film before her death in 1995.

Little Women is an autobiographical novel about Louisa May Alcott, her three sisters, and her parents. The lives of the four sisters were mostly based on real events, including how Beth caught her illness from helping near-destitute family, the fact that the Alcotts lived in poverty, and the need for the younger members of the family to work to support the household.

Amy is based on the youngest of the Alcott Sisters, Abigail "May" Alcott Nieriker. Also a passionate artist, she illustrated the first edition of the book. Alcott and her sister May rarely got along well and would have bitter fights, just like Jo and Amy. I've seen various articles that say, "Amy is the March sister that most readers love to hate"[52] and that she is "literally the worst."[53] The reason why she's my least favorite is that she burns Jo's only draft of the first book she wrote. It almost seems like Alcott is punishing her sister through writing the character of Amy (unless May was exactly like Amy, and if so, yikes!).

There were divergences between the book and real life. The biggest departure was that Louisa May Alcott served as a nurse during the Civil War during her 30s, so the family members were quite a bit older during that time than they were portrayed in the book. Her mother was the main breadwinner of the family, and one of the first social workers in the U.S.

Interestingly, some parts of the movie were not pulled from the book but from Alcott's life. Arguably the most important instance of this was that I could find no mention of anything related to transcendentalism in the book, but from my research I found that it was the guiding light for Alcott's family, especially her father, who devoted his life to the cause.

---

[52] Shmoop Editorial Team 2008
[53] Keely 2017

CHAPTER 22: Contact (1997)

CAST:

Jodie Foster—Eleanor "Ellie" Arroway

Matthew McConaughey—Palmer Joss

Tom Skerritt—David Drumlin

David Morse—Ted Arroway

Jena Malone—Young Ellie

William Fichtner—Kent

DIRECTED BY:

Robert Zemeckis

WRITING CREDITS:

Screenplay by: James V. Hart and Michael Goldenberg

Based on the novel *Contact* by: Carl Sagan

Based on the story by: Carl Sagan and Ann Druyan

Plot Summary

Ellie Arroway has wanted to be an astronomer since she was 8 years old, partly due to spending endless hours peering at the stars through a telescope, and partly due to the encouragement of her father and his knowledge of astronomy. She was very close to him, especially because her mother had died when Ellie was younger. When her father dies of a heart attack when she is 9, she is devastated and becomes an orphan.

She pours all of herself into becoming a brilliant astronomer. Her mission is to find intelligent life on other planets, so she takes a job with the Search for Extraterrestrial Life Institute (SETI) at the Arecibo Observatory in Puerto Rico. This is where she meets her beloved teammates, including Kent, who will help her more than she would have ever anticipated.

After the team loses the funding for their research, Ellie finds a billionaire backer and starts over at the Very Large Array Radio Telescope facility in New Mexico with her team. There she hears an audio message sent by aliens, coming from the star Vega. As more of the message is revealed, Ellie must fight both a love interest and a pompous scientist to stay part of the project and possibly explore life on other planets.

My Thoughts on This Movie

I remember that when I first watched the beginning of the movie I thought it was one of the most beautiful things I had ever seen. It starts with showing Earth from space, then the shot pans out through the solar system, the Milky Way, several other galaxies and finally through the wider universe. It's all done through the CGI of the '90s, which to me is more beautiful and more realistic than the CGI we have today. (I'm not alone, at least in the realism department, as I've seen many pieces and videos online about how and why this is true.)

Watching this scene reminds me of my reaction to the mind-blowing visual effects in *Jurassic Park*. When I saw it in the theater when it first came out, I was blown away by the dinosaurs. Watching that movie gave me a shivering feeling of delight, to see something that looked so realistic that logically couldn't be real.

Just like in *Jurassic Park*, when I first watched *Contact* I felt delighted by watching a sci-fi movie come so believably to life. There are a lot of other lovely CGI effects throughout the movie. They didn't overwhelm me, but instead lead me to be more fully immersed in the movie.

One of the things I saw in Ellie was how she kept her childlike wonder and curiosity her entire life. Being an orphan at age 9 could have completely snuffed this out. I strive to be like Ellie. I see the world and everyone and everything in it as a place to explore throughout my lifetime. Unlike Ellie, I don't have any gifts for the hard sciences. My strengths lie in the social sciences and the humanities. I find people more fascinating than the cosmos. However, I did find the aliens in this movie intriguing.

I feel that the romance between the love interest, Palmer Joss, and Ellie is refreshing. It seems rooted in reality and is really a subplot of the movie. It's not shown as important that Ellie finds a man. Instead, in the world of the movie, the focus of this subplot is on how important it is to have someone who makes a good companion, who supports you, and who makes an excellent equal. There are many movies in which women are supposedly working too hard, but when they develop a relationship, they become "better" people and find the perfect work/life balance. Ellie is never shamed for being so dedicated to her work.

One of the most interesting themes in the movie is what happens when science, religion, and politics meet. Ellie believes in science above all things and does not believe in a higher power. She feels that religion has no part in science and those who try to interject a higher power into her most sacred of subjects are deluded.

She tries to convert Palmer into atheism through using logic, but it doesn't work. Palmer, though, believes in a higher power and thinks that since Ellie doesn't, she may not be fit to represent all humankind when it comes to first contact with aliens. Neither Ellie nor Palmer are interested in political games.

The pompous scientist I mentioned in the plot summary, David Drumlin, is most interested in using science, religion, and politics so he can gather as much power and glory as possible, no matter the cost to anyone else. At least according to Ellie, he will spout off about his belief in God when he thinks it's to his best advantage.

How Watching This Movie Can Affect Our Mental Health

Watching movies where the main character's passion is their work and seeing them happily toil countless hours towards some kind of goal or goals can make me feel less than by comparison. I feel embarrassed about how hard it can be with my mental health issues to even work full time. What I do, if I am able, is remind myself of what I have accomplished and that everyone's journey is different. If I wasn't taking care of my mental health and putting it first, I know things would get 10 times worse. I know this to be true from years of experience.

Do you ever wish that you could do more in your life, but feel hampered by mild to severe mental and/or physical health issues? Do you feel that you don't have as much passion as others, or that you aren't working hard enough to reach your goals? I encourage you to think about what you are doing well in your life.

It doesn't matter if what you are doing well is surviving each day, working on your coping skills, finding a bit of passion here and there, or loving people you care about. You are doing something with your life. Don't push yourself too hard. We don't all have to be constantly pursuing some big passion to find meaning in our lives.

There are a lot of wonderfully eccentric characters in this film. There's a good deal of talk about how strange Ellie is in some ways, including from those who care about her. Some of her teammates can be out there—at least at times. Her billionaire backer is very odd. In the world of the movie, these characters aren't flawed because of their eccentricity. Instead, each character's weirdness is a gift. They are made for each other because they are all a little strange.

This is definitely true for me and many of my friends—we are good together because we don't try to be the type of people society thinks we should be. This is important to me as that's how I want to see myself. If you are also a bit weird and you want to feel more accepted and awesome, watch this movie.

Caveats and Triggers

A possible trigger: having someone die in front of you when you thought you could have saved them if you did something differently.

Fun Facts

The star Vega, where the alien message comes from, is 25 light-years away. It is a beautiful blue color and can be seen by the naked eye. There are many myths about Vega, but I found this one particularly lovely:

"In Japan, Vega is called Orihime, a celestial princess or goddess. She falls in love with a mortal, Hikoboshi, represented by the star Altair. But when Orihime's father finds out, he is enraged and forbids her to see this mere mortal… The two lovers are placed in the sky, separated by the Celestial River or Milky Way. Yet the sky gods are kind, and they reunite on the 7th night of the 7th moon each year. Sometimes Hikoboshi's annual trip across the Celestial River is treacherous, though, and he doesn't make it. In that case, Orihime's tears form raindrops that fall over Japan."[54]

The movie is based on astronomer Carl Sagan's book of the same name. He spent much of his career trying to prove that there was extraterrestrial life somewhere in the universe. I have read his book many times and, like the movie, it is fascinating and powerful. He was a huge part of the making of the movie but died during production, devastating not only his family and friends, but also everyone who worked on the movie and his multitudes of fans. At the end of the movie, you will see the words "For Carl."

Roger Ebert compiled a list of over 300 films that he considered "great." Two of the movies in this book, *Contact* and *Eternal Sunshine of the Spotless Mind* (see Chapter 12), are on this list. Ebert had this to say in his review:

"The strength of 'Contact' is in the way it engages in issues that are relevant today, and still only rarely discussed in the movies. Consider the opposition to stem cell research, which in a sense is 'pure research.' Consider the politicians who disparage separation of church and state. When Ellie was asked by Congress if she believed in God, the correct reply would have

---

[54] Sessions 2018

been, 'that is none of your business.' That would have been the correct reply of any American, no matter whether they believed in God or not."[55]

[55] Ebert 2011

CONCLUSION

So, I'm sad to say, it's time to wrap up. I can't tell you how much I've enjoyed writing this book, and I'm excited about sharing my experiences watching these movies with you. I hope that reading this book brings you comfort and leads you to new discoveries about yourself and others.

As I discussed in Chapter 3, I went through training to be a peer support specialist so I could help people with their mental health issues. I worked in that capacity for a year. Through training, I learned how to use shared experience to help others on their mental health journey.

So, in this book I share the details of my experience: how I discovered through the training that it was better for me to watch movies and truly engage with them instead of engaging in destructive coping skills. Therefore, I hope that you may find that replacing even one of your more destructive coping skills with watching movies is ultimately better for your mental health.

Of course, like any human, I still do things that aren't good for my physical, spiritual, and emotional health. I also want to make clear that as long as they aren't harming others, I don't judge others for any actions that can possibly damage or lessen them in some way. I would also note that I am not trying to tell you which films you "should" or "shouldn't" watch. I've recently watched and will probably continue to watch movies that have a significant ick factor. I do agree with cinematherapist Gary Solomon that watching certain violent movies can still benefit the viewer.

I'll give you an example. Remember how I talked about how a woman who was interviewed stated that she was still shaken by a movie in *The Hunger Games* series even after viewing it? Still with me? Good.

In July 2018, I lost my beloved dog Charlie, and in the first 24 hours after his death I was just numb. I wanted to cry, but I couldn't. I remembered how Birgit Wolz wrote about how when she couldn't cry after her stroke, she thought to watch movies that would likely move her to cry. So, I rewatched the first film in *The Hunger Games* series.

If you haven't seen it or read the books, it's set in a dystopian future U.S., which is now called Panem. All power and wealth are contained in the capital of

Panem, and every year the 12 districts of Panem are required to send one boy and one girl from each district to fight to the death with only one victor out of 24 remaining alive at the end. Katniss Everdeen is the protagonist, and when her little sister is randomly chosen to be sent to the fight to the death called "The Hunger Games," Katniss volunteers to go in her stead. I always cry during this scene. The raw emotions including fear and anger are on full display and seeing and hearing these emotions gets me.

Still, the extreme violence throughout the movie affects me every time. So, it's ultimately a tradeoff, as is any movie that you might have reservations about. All I'm really trying to say here is to proceed with caution while being open to any possibilities of healing. Trust your gut when you know of or encounter an ick factor. You know best about what's okay to put into your brain.

What binds the 12 movies in this book together? They all help my mental health in some way and have low to zero ick factor. What I haven't told you yet is something else: they *all* have at least one character I can strongly relate to, and at least one that I aspire to be like—and sometimes these characters overlap. Here are some examples (most of which I touched on earlier in the book):

As a writer, I identify with Jo in *Little Women* and aspire to write amazing books and stories like her. One of my aims in life is to be like Julia in *Defending Your Life*, to be in the moment, to take chances, and live my best life. I already am as silly and full of wonder as she is. I believe I am as empathetic as Sadness is in *Inside Out*. I aspire to be even a fraction as impactful to society as Ellie in *Contact*. I would love to be as loyal, clever, and kind as Fezzik in *The Princess Bride*, and I like to think I'm almost there in at least cleverness and kindness. I identify with Joel and Clementine in *Eternal Sunshine of The Spotless Mind* as I can be quiet, introspective, and anxious, yet also boisterous, free-spirited, and friendly.

I would encourage you to do what I do when watching a movie; think about which characters you are like and which you aspire to be. I got the idea to home in on this concept from cinematherapist Birgit Wolz (see Chapter 6), and it's really been helpful for me.

I'll leave you with the answer to why I titled this book *Our Favorite Movies*. The answer is three-fold: first, I'm guessing that many of you will consider at least one of these movies as a favorite (I'm betting on *The Princess Bride* for the most votes), second, several of these are movies my sister and I loved to watch together, and third, I would be honored if, after reading the book, you watch one or more of these movies for the first time and they become ones you fiercely love.

ACKNOWLEDGMENTS

I'm a little anxious here—what order am I supposed to thank people in? I've seen different ways in different books. I guess I'll just have to wing it.

First, without the help of my book coach and editor, Amy Collette, it would have taken me much longer to finish the book, if I could have pulled it off at all. The clarity and focus she brought to the editing are much appreciated. She is one of the kindest, most grounding and supportive people I know. She gently but firmly guided me through this process.

Thanks to Melody Christian for creating my spectacular front and back covers. She was infinitely patient with me through the design process, especially when it came to things like my finicky obsession with the "perfect" fonts.

Next, I want to thank my beta readers: my parents Joyce and Bruce Feustel, my aunt Donna Eder, my sister Jane Feustel Bensimhon, and my friend Lena Lund. Multiple big shout outs to Lena for: being the only nonfamily member to beta read, being so thorough in her feedback, putting a lot of care into the process, and being one of my favorite people.

I also want to thank everyone who has nerded out over movies with me. This is such a long list of people

I could not put even a fraction of their names in here. Thank you to those who love quoting movies back and forth with me. Thank you to the people who have recommended movies to me that I love. Thank you to all my friends who have told me specifically why they love the movies that made it into the book. All I have to do is say the words "The Princess Bride" and the love pours out of people.

Thanks to all my friends who support me, laugh with me, help me feel not so alone, encourage me, and watch movies with me. Special thanks to my best friend Sara Lewis, my favorite roomie ever, one of the smartest and funniest people I know, and one heck of a mom to two wonderful girls.

I wouldn't have been able to write this without the professionals who do their best to assist me with my physical and mental health. Special shout out to my acupuncturist, Kay.

Thank you to everyone who helped create each of the 12 movies in this book.

I want to thank the following people who have written eloquently about mental health: Jenny Lawson, Susanna Kaysen, Sylvia Plath, Allie Brosh, Ellen Forney, Lori Schiller, Oliver Sacks, Birgit Wolz, Gary Solomon, Scott Stossel, Carrie Fisher, and Kay Redfield Jamison. Special shout out to Jenny Lawson, who makes me laugh and feel understood more than any other writer. She is a big influence, especially when it comes to her hilarious digressions which often are set off by parentheses.

I want to thank my sister, niece, mom, and dad from the bottom of my heart. Jane, thanks for being my movie buddy, for your kindness, and being part of my support system. Hava, thanks for being a thoughtful, silly, and inquisitive niece. Mom, thanks for inspiring me to write my heart out, for your unending optimism, for helping me to be a better editor and proofreader, and all the ways you helped me with the book. Dad, thanks for your humor, for being there for me in every possible way, and for teaching me empathy.

Finally, thanks to my best furry friend Bogie, who is always ready for a cuddle. His purr is so loud that I am convinced I could hear it from outer space.

RESOURCES

Brosh, Allie — *Hyperbole and a Half: Unfortunate Situations, Flawed Coping Mechanisms, Mayhem, and Other Things That Happened*

Fisher, Carrie — *Wishful Drinking*

Forney, Ellen — *Marbles: Mania, Depression, Michelangelo and Me*

Jamison, Kay Redfield — *An Unquiet Mind: A Memoir of Moods and Madness*

Kaysen, Susanna — *Girl, Interrupted*

Lawson, Jenny — *Furiously Happy: A Funny Book About Horrible Things*
Let's Pretend This Never Happened

Plath, Sylvia — *The Bell Jar*

Schiller, Lori — *The Quiet Room: A Journey Out of the Torment of Madness*

Solomon, Gary — *The Motion Picture Prescription: Watch This Movie and Call Me in the Morning*
Reel Therapy: How Movies Inspire You to Overcome Life's Problems
Cinemaparenting: Using Movies to Teach Life's Most Important Lessons

Stossel, Scott — *My Age of Anxiety: Fear, Hope, Dread, and the Search for Peace of Mind*

Wolz, Birgit — *E-Motion Picture Magic: A Movie Lover's Guide to Healing and Transformation*

REFERENCES

Behavioral Tech. (2018). What is Dialectical Behavior Therapy
(DBT)? *Behavioral Tech.* Retrieved from
https://behavioraltech.org/resources/faqs/dialectical-
behavior-therapy-dbt/

Berman, E. (2015). Meet the Real Women Who Inspired *A League
of Their Own. Time.* Retrieved from
http://time.com/3760024/women-professional-baseball/

Buckmaster, L. (2018). Crocodile Dundee was sexist, racist and
homophobic. Let's not bring that back. *The Guardian.*
Retrieved from
https://www.theguardian.com/film/2018/jan/23/crocodil
e-dundee-was-sexist-racist-and-homophobic-lets-not-bring-
that-back

Cinematherapy.com. (2018). What experts say about cinema
therapy. Retrieved from
http://www.cinematherapy.com/experts.html

Cline, R. (2017). Michael Caine: Comedy is 'Harder' than Drama.
Contactmusic.com. Retrieved from
http://www.contactmusic.com/michael-
caine/news/michael-caine-comedy-is-hard_5643305

Colorado Mental Wellness Network. (2018). Peer Support Specialist
Training with CMWN. Colorado Mental Wellness
Network. Retrieved from
https://coloradomentalwellnessnetwork.org/recovery-
education/peer-support-specialist/

Dumtrache, S.D. (2014). The Effects of a Cinema-therapy Group on
Diminishing Anxiety in Young People. *Procedia - Social and
Behavioral Sciences, 127.* Retrieved from
https://www.sciencedirect.com/science/article/pii/S1877
042814024331

Duncan, J. & Fordham, J. (2016). Eternal Sunshine of the Spotless
Mind's Surreal Effects. *Tested.* Retrieved from
http://www.tested.com/art/movies/572271-eternal-
sunshine-spotless-minds-surreal-effects/

Ebert, R. (1990). Joe Versus the Volcano. Retrieved from
https://www.rogerebert.com/reviews/joe-versus-the-
volcano-1990

Ebert, R. (1995). Tommy Boy. Retrieved from
https://www.rogerebert.com/reviews/tommy-boy-1995

Ebert, R. (2011). Contact. Retrieved from
https://www.rogerebert.com/reviews/great-movie-
contact-1997

el Kaliouby, R. (2015). Inside Out sparks a dialogue around
emotions. *Affectiva.* Retrieved from
http://blog.affectiva.com/inside-out-sparks-a-dialogue-
around-emotions

Firstenberg, J.P. (2005). AFI's 100 Years...100 Movie Quotes. *AFI.*
Retrieved from http://www.afi.com/100years/quotes.aspx

Henne, B.G. (2015). Here's how special effects were made for
Eternal Sunshine of The Spotless Mind. AV News. Retrieved
from https://news.avclub.com/here-s-how-special-effects-
were-made-for-eternal-sunshi-1798280308

Hicks, M. (2018). Antecedents of New Thought: Ralph Waldo
Emerson. Retrieved from
https://www.truthunity.net/lessons/mark-
hicks/background-of-new-thought/ralph-waldo-emerson

IMDB. (2018). Fried Green Tomatoes. *IMDB.* Retrieved from
http://www.imdb.com/title/tt0101921/trivia

Janicke, S.H. (2016). How Positive Media Can Make Us Better
People. *Greater Good Magazine.* Retrieved from
https://greatergood.berkeley.edu/article/item/how_positi
ve_media_can_make_us_better_people

Keely. (2017). Why Amy March From Little Women is Literally the Worst. *Buzzfeed.* Retrieved from https://www.buzzfeed.com/angharadpiano/why-amy-march-from-little-women-is-literally-the-w-11peo?utm_term=.qdDBa11BZK#.jk05jdd5PJ

Lee, Y. & Yang, H. (2005). The use of single-session cinematherapy and aggressive behavioral tendencies among adopted children—A pilot study. *American Journal of Recreation Therapy.* Retrieved from http://www.calvin.edu/~yl33/documents/Yang.pdf

Lo, M. (2008). A Quickie with Mary-Louise Parker. *AfterEllen.com.* Retrieved from http://www.afterellen.com/tv/35232-a-quickie-with-mary-louise-parker

Mann, D. (2007) Movie Therapy: Using Movies for Mental Health. *WebMD.* Retrieved from https://www.webmd.com/mental-health/features/movie-therapy-using-movies-for-mental-health

Marsick, E. (2010). Cinematherapy with preadolescents experiencing parental divorce: A collective case study. *The Arts in Psychotherapy.* pp 311–318 Retrieved from https://www.sciencedirect.com/science/article/abs/pii/S0197455610000687

Mottram, J. (2013). Samuel L Jackson: Tarantino, racism and the N-word. *Independent.* Retrieved from https://www.independent.co.uk/arts-entertainment/films/features/samuel-l-jackson-tarantino-racism-and-the-n-word-8452821.html

Oswalt, P. (2015). *Silver Screen Fiend: Learning About Life from an Addiction to Film.* New York, NY: Scribner.

Oxford English Dictionary. (2018). Retrieved from https://en.oxforddictionaries.com/definition/transcendentalism

Pozios, V.K., Kambam, P.R., & Bender, H.E. (2013). Does Media Violence Lead to the Real Thing? *The New York Times.* Retrieved from https://www.nytimes.com/2013/08/25/opinion/sunday/does-media-violence-lead-to-the-real-thing.html

Schnelbach, L. (2017). The Unlikely Philosophy of *Joe Versus the Volcano. Tor.com.* Retrieved from https://www.tor.com/2017/02/20/the-unlikely-philosophy-of-joe-versus-the-volcano/

Sessions, L. (2018). Happy Chinese Valentine's Day, from Vega. *EarthSky.* Retrieved from https://earthsky.org/brightest-stars/vega-brilliant-blue-white-is-third-brightest-star

Shakespeare Theatre Company. (2018). The Comedy of Errors. *Shakespeare Theatre Company.* Retrieved from http://www.shakespearetheatre.org/events/comedy-errors-18-19/

Shmoop Editorial Team. (2008). Amy March in Little Women. Retrieved https://www.shmoop.com/little-women/amy-march.html

Solomon, G. (1995). *The Motion Picture Prescription: Watch This Movie and Call Me in the Morning.* Fairfield, CT: Aslan Publishing.

Solomon, G. (2001). *Reel Therapy: How Movies Inspire You to Overcome Life's Problems.* New York, NY: Lebhar-Friedman Books. Digital.

Suskind, R. (2014). *Life, Animated: A Story of Sidekicks, Heroes, and Autism.* Glendale, CA: Kingswell.

Terrero, N. (2015). Inside Out: Phyllis Smith had no clue Sadness would be prominent character. *Entertainment Weekly.* Retrieved from http://ew.com/article/2015/10/12/phyllis-smith-inside-out-sadness/

Totten, S. (2014). New research explains why movies make us feel strong emotions. *Southern California Public Radio.* Retrieved from https://www.scpr.org/news/2014/12/04/48457/what-watching-movies-can-tell-us-about-how-our-bra/

USHistory.org. (2018). Transcendentalism, An American Philosophy. *U.S. History Online Textbook.* Retrieved from http://www.ushistory.org/us/26f.asp

Williams, A. (2010). Real-Life "League of Their Own:" Remembering Dottie. *Ms. Magazine.* http://msmagazine.com/blog/2010/05/25/real-life-league-of-their-own-remembering-player-dottie-kamenshek/

Wolz, B. (2004). *E-Motion Picture Magic: A Movie Lover's Guide to Healing and Transformation.* Centennial, CO: Glenbridge Publishing Ltd.

Wolz, B. (2018). Fried Green Tomatoes. Retrieved from http://www.cinematherapy.com/birgitarticles/Fried%20Green%20Tomatoes.html

Wong, D. (2012). 5 Ways You Don't Realize Movies Are Controlling Your Brain. *Cracked.com.* Retrieved from http://www.cracked.com/blog/5-ways-you-dont-realize-movies-are-controlling-your-brain/

Wood, J. (2016). 'Defending Your Life' at 25: Albert Brooks on Making a Comedy Classic. *Rolling Stone.* https://www.rollingstone.com/movies/movie-news/defending-your-life-at-25-albert-brooks-on-making-a-comedy-classic-178596/

TheDivineBetteMidler. (January 4, 2013). Bette Midler - Good Morning America 1988 (Big Business Interview). Retrieved from https://www.youtube.com/watch?v=nxqgGgP7df4

ABOUT THE AUTHOR

Anne Feustel, the owner of Writing Wisely, works as an editor, proofreader, writer, blogger, and content creator. After writing a play at age 7 about a character in Mister Rogers' Neighborhood, she caught the writing bug. With a B.A. in Sociology and a minor in Psychology, Anne is uniquely qualified to write about the human experience.

Because she has dealt with mental health issues since she was a child, and felt called to working with others with the same issues, Anne wants to help find easily accessible ways to improve everyone's mental health.

She enjoys watching cat videos, spending time with furry friends, enjoying movies, stamping out mental health stigma, and being an avid reader. Anne lives in

Lakewood, Colorado with her cat, Bogie. This is her first book.

Connect with Anne at her website wearewritingwisely.com and her Facebook page Writing Wisely.